From the reviews of
RECOVERING AMERICAN LITERATURE...

"My hunch is that Shaw's jeremiad, for all its intensity and eminent good sense, will fall on English departments now filled to over-flowing with dead ears."—Sanford Pinsker, *American Literature*

"Lucid and impressive...a well-written, thoroughly researched, and much needed book.—John P. Sisk, *American Scholar*

"In charting the disintegration of intellectual discussion of several of the nation's (and the world's) great books, *Recovering American Literature* proves that when criticism ceases to be an open forum of ideas centered on a text and emanating from that text's rich store of ambiguity and ambivalence, it does indeed become vulgar." —Loxley F. Nichols. *Chronicles*

"Reading Shaw's book may be painful for what it reveals about the sad state of contemporary criticism, but, as his title implies, be-coming aware of what has gone wrong in the literary academy today is the necessary first step to 'recovering American literature' and indeed all of our cultural heritage."—Paul A. Cantor, *The Public Interest*

"At its best, criticism is a philosophical journey. At its worst, as this interesting book shows us, in today's universities it's a bull session in the remedial reading class."—Katherine Knorr, *International Herald-Tribune*

"There is something inherently ridiculous about the spectacle of literature professors poring grimly over 19th-century novels to determine how strictly they adhere to the tenets of political cor-rectness. But as is amply demonstrated in Peter Shaw's valuable book, the humor of the situation is lost on the professors them-selves."—Evelyn Toynton, *Commentary*

"Devastating....It's a book to make you weep, when it doesn't make you hoot with laughter."—Roger Miller, *Milwaukee Journal*

Recovering American Literature

PETER SHAW

ELEPHANT PAPERBACKS
Ivan R. Dee, Publisher, Chicago

RECOVERING AMERICAN LITERATURE. Copyright © 1994 by
Peter Shaw.
This book was first published in 1994 by Ivan R. Dee.

First ELEPHANT PAPERBACK edition published 1995 by
Ivan R. Dee, Inc., 1332 North Halsted Street, Chicago 60622.
Manufactured in the United States of America and printed
on acid-free paper.

Library of Congress Cataloging-in-Publication Data:
Shaw, Peter, 1936–
Recovering American literature / Peter Shaw.
p. cm.
"Elephant paperbacks."
Includes bibliographical references and index.
ISBN 1-56663-095-9
1. American literature—19th century—History and criticism—
Theory, etc. 2. Criticism—United States—History—20th century.
3. Literature and history—United States—History.
4. Canon (Literature) I. Title.
[PS201.S48   1995]
810.9′003—dc20   95-32552

Once again, for Penny

ACKNOWLEDGMENTS

FOR PIONEERING THE intellectual approach to critical trends that I have adopted, my thanks to Kenneth Lynn and my former colleague, Richard Levin. John Thompson, Frederick Brown, Kenneth Silverman, and Neal Kozodoy have been encouraging readers, and Jane Uscilka of *Partisan Review* a particularly helpful editor. Thanks, as in the past, to the journal editors—Staige Blackford, Joseph Epstein, William Phillips, and Edith Kurzweil—who published the following chapters in somewhat different form: "*Moby-Dick*" as "Cutting a Classic Down to Size," *Virginia Quarterly Review* (Winter 1993); "*Billy Budd*" as "The Fate of a Story," *American Scholar* (Autumn 1993); "*Huckleberry Finn*" as "The Genteel Fate of *Huckleberry Finn*," *Partisan Review* (Summer 1993). "*Typee*" appeared as "Civilization and Its Malcontents: Responses to *Typee*," *New Criterion* (January 1985), and in my *The War Against the Intellect: Episodes in the Decline of Discourse* (Ames, Iowa, 1989).

Jeff Finlay helped with two years of research and typing, the first year of which was paid for by funds attached to the Will and Ariel Durant Professorship of Humanities which I held at St. Peter's College, Jersey City (1990–1991). Other expenses during research and preparation of the manuscript were generously paid for by the Historical Research Foundation. The chapter on *Billy Budd* benefited from exchanges with students and professors when it was delivered as a talk at Princeton University and to the Committee on Social Thought, University of Chicago.

Research was conducted at the Columbia University libraries, the library of St. Peter's College, the New York Public Library, the New York University Bobst Library, and the Library of Congress.

Finally, thanks to Doctors Henry Greenberg, Oscar Garfein, Stephen Scheidt, Milton Packer, Chin Yeoh, Ronald Kraft, and Stephan Lynn who, along with my wife Penny, have resourcefully kept me alive and able to work.

CONTENTS

Recovering American Literature

INTRODUCTION

THE ATTITUDES OF American critics toward the classic American novels of the nineteenth century underwent a transformation after the 1960s. From the 1920s through the 1960s critics emphasized the distinctive qualities of American writing. They identified the moralizing bent whereby, in a troubled and troubling way, American authors probed the ultimate meanings of life and society. And they explored the tendency in the same authors toward indirect, symbolic expression of their doubts about the meaning of it all. In contrast, since the 1960s critics have become convinced that not metaphysical doubt but political certainty characterized the same nineteenth-century writers. American literature was an outright assault on specific failings of American society: racism, sexism, homophobia, economic exploitation, class oppression, and imperialism. The literature's preoccupations, this is to say, exactly matched those of academic radicalism from the 1960s to the present.

"In the last decade," Gerald Graff could write in 1986 of a trend that has continued since then, "virtually every phase of American literature has been reinterpreted in political terms." Specifically, as Sacvan Bercovitch put it more recently, "the subversive in literature has been raised to the transcendent status once reserved for the noble, the tragic, and the complex."[1] American literature has been Marxified, these two critics are admitting. Politics, and specifically the politics of subversion, has become more important than anything else. Accordingly, criticism has devolved into a search for subversion in the classic American works, which are now judged according to how well they reward this search.

A number of observers have remarked on the dubiousness of such a change in critical values. Frederick Crews lists the "liabilities" of the politicizing approach as "its self-righteousness, its tendency to conceive of American history only as a highlight film of outrages, its impatience with artistic purposes other than 'redefining the social order,' and its choice of critical principles according to the partisan cause at hand." Sacvan Bercovitch remarks that in reading politicized criticism "we come to feel" that "the American ideology is a system of ideas in the service of evil." Barbara Foley, who believes exactly this about America, nevertheless finds that her fellow ideologizers deceive themselves when they write about literature. She accuses them of letting their "own brand of oppositional politics" become "conflated with authorial intention." That is, ideologizers confuse the author's opinions with their own so that works of the past "frequently take on an aura of anachronistic political correctness."[2]

Some of the critics Foley describes recognize this anachronism but defend its political utility. They are concerned not so much with what an author creates as with how his story can be manipulated to yield correct views. So if Hawthorne from their viewpoint insufficiently emphasized and failed to endorse his character Hester Prynne's feminist impulses, today's critic can read *The Scarlet Letter* as though he had. For example, Jonathan Arac addresses himself to ideologizing critics who share his wish that Hawthorne had created a more politically radical Hester. "We must," he instructs them, "confront Hawthorne's failure to actualize" such a Hester. The critic can then "construct" the Hester he wants. Following Arac's "scheme" of interpretation whereby characters are treated "as projections of ideological possibilities," the critic can transform Hawthorne into what he should have been: "a fundamentally subversive writer."[3]

The critic Alfred Habegger, in writing about Henry James, uses the word "historicizing" to describe essentially the same scheme. Judith Fetterly, preparing to make James's *The Bostonians* come out the way she would prefer, more straightforwardly admits that her scheme amounts to unleashing her own "subjectivity."[4] Other critics have still other terms, but everywhere the outcome is the same: one way or another the American classics are made to serve political ends.

Yet whatever contemporary critics do to bring about the fictional outcomes they desire, they express resentment and dismay when authors fail to see things their way in the first place. These authors must be artistic as well as political failures, the critics conclude, and they proceed to search for defects of plotting, characterization, narration, and the use of dialogue. In the end it emerges that the critics have by and large come not to like American literature. They therefore present the spectacle of a national literature that stands condemned on aesthetic and moral grounds by the very people who have chosen to devote their professional lives to it.

The academics in question have neither experience nor standing when it comes to the aesthetic evaluation of literature. But empowered as they are by their political allegiances, they exude an air of authority in these matters. And such is the institutional strength of their position that they are not to be gainsaid by anyone who doubts their judgments. One might have expected, for example, that the exposé of their confusions delivered by the politically radical Barbara Foley would have come from traditionalist scholars of American literature. Or that Gerald Graff and Sacvan Bercovitch would have accompanied their descriptions of politicized criticism with some expression of dismay at its advent. Instead, older, traditional critics have in fact largely remained silent or acquiescent. Despite the politicizers' own designation of themselves as politically radical revisionists, their colleagues blandly treat them as serving a literary movement fundamentally no different from any other. As for those few older critics who are willing to acknowledge the politics of revisionism—as Bercovitch and Crews do, for example—they maintain that whatever its proponents' aims may be, these do not pose a threat to the overall critical enterprise.

Yet the very proliferation of denials that a radical gauntlet has been thrown down points to the disingenuousness of older critics. Radical revisionism is manifestly not the familiar challenge to established literary interpretations they describe. Instead it is a movement dedicated to the exposure and denunciation of political wrongdoing. Whoever resists revisionism's new interpretations, therefore, finds that he is regarded not as disputing literary points but rather as demonstrating moral insensitivity by rejecting a noble attempt to right the ills of society. Not surprisingly, few critics have been willing to face such a charge: the sanguine attitude professed by most academics is really the product of intimidation.

This intimidation is built into the politicizing argument. For who, that argument implies, but the morally insensitive—or the outright racist—could fail to concentrate on the racial issue rather than the comedy of *Huckleberry Finn*? Who but a misogynist or patriarchal phallocentrist could presume to judge as in any sense guilty Hester Prynne, the cruelly treated, helpless young woman of *The Scarlet Letter*? And who but a militarist or indeed a fascist could find reasons to defend the decision of Billy Budd's captain to order his hanging? Lest anyone doubt the consequences of dissenting from the politically correct attitude on each of these questions, the hectoring, self-righteous tone of today's criticism noted by Frederick Crews clearly signals what can be expected. So do the attacks on one another by the politicizing critics, who stifle deviationism with what Gerald Graff has described as "accusatory ideological terminology."[5]

In the resultant atmosphere of intimidation, scholarly observers of the new politicization have either remained silent or taken pains not to offend. An annual review of critical writings on American literature assures its readers that the book *Marxist Models of Literary Realism* is "well written and not doctrinaire." The "Marxist perspective" of another critic is one "forcing us to rethink many basic assumptions about our American heritage." Judith Fetterly's *The Resisting Reader: A Feminist Approach to American Literature* is "ideological and mildly polemical, but it is well written, thoughtful, and convincing." Lillian S. Robinson's essay collection *Sex, Class, and Culture* "provides fresh insights into familiar subjects."[6]

Older critics, when they have been directly attacked by radical revisionists, have sometimes defended themselves, but typically they refrain from any discussion of the direction being taken by American criticism. A partial exception is Hyatt Waggoner's objection to the caricatured ways in which three younger critics' books on Hawthorne described his generation's treatment of *The Scarlet Letter*. In a review written in 1978 the eminent Hawthornian scholar regarded such caricature as an "ominous" professional development.[7]

Waggoner's contemporaries, though, have tended to make peace with their attackers.

Henry Nash Smith, for example, repeatedly apologized in his last years for his classic study of the symbolism of the American West, *Virgin Land* (1950). Sacvan Bercovitch, for whose aptly titled anthology *Ideology and Classic American Literature* Smith supplied one of his recantations, elliptically but compellingly referred to the pressures on older scholars like Smith. "Smith's essay," Bercovitch wrote, "is eloquent and exemplary in its recognition of the ideological dimensions of scholarship." So it was. Expressing himself in the party-line language of someone who has just emerged from a reeducation camp, Smith confessed his guilt. "I did not realize," "I did not at least glance at . . . ," I was guilty of "an emotional contagion," "I had in this fashion lost the capacity for facing up to the tragic dimensions of the Westward Movement"—all this of a work that looms gigantically above anything written by Smith's ideological detractors.[8]

A few academics in the generation after Smith's, without necessarily agreeing with all the critical judgments of his generation, at least continue to honor its canons of logic. But their writing and reviewing has become a study in rueful accommodation, including supplying congratulatory blurbs and approving reviews for radically revisionist books. Among critics of this generation direct challenges to the reigning orthodoxy are rare. Only Kenneth Lynn, David Hirsch, and to some extent Frederick Crews have challenged the post-1960s politicizing consensus.

Among younger critics some few occasionally adopt a traditional opinion. But as David Hirsch has observed, their defensive, apologetic way of doing so exposes "the coercive nature of the new orthodoxy that is settling into the academy." Even a critic whom one would have thought sufficiently wrapped in the mantle of "theory" to be safe from attack, displays uneasiness over so much as reporting an American author's opinion of a kind presently regarded as unorthodox. In discussing *Billy Budd* this critic apologizes for doing Melville a "disservice" by revealing, as Hirsch pointedly understates it, Melville's opinion that "the brutal excesses of the French Revolution were not an unmitigated good."[9]

Clearly, the free discussion of American literature is being stifled by a new, radical orthodoxy. For the grip of this orthodoxy to be loosened, its coerciveness and its damaging effects on literature need to be systematically exposed. When they are, it quickly becomes apparent that the skewed interpretations now in favor are not actually new. They go back to the 1950s, when they were given a hearing but judged to be minor contributions worthy of no more than passing mention. At that time the interpreters, usually Marxists, admitted their partiality and contented themselves with seeking out the places where American writers were critical of American society and government. They never went so far as to claim that politics either exhausted the implications of the American classics or lent them their distinctive qualities. Nor were they prepared to distort literary interpretation in the service of politics.

It was not and is not necessary for critics to impose their ideologies on works of literature. After all, critics are perfectly free to express their own preferences. It is not necessary, for example, to satisfy one's own politically radical or fellow-traveling allegiance by making Melville out to have been an enthusiast of the French Revolution he loathed. The radical critic Myra Jehlen manages to discuss Melville without either distorting his intentions or compromising her own views. "The impact of *Billy Budd*, as of *Moby Dick* and of *Pierre*," she writes, "may be to make *us* rebel (though only some of us) but it is against Melville's despair rather than in response to his vision. For even Melville had blinded himself rather than see beyond America."[10] Here is a straightforward, politically motivated avowal that cannot be faulted on literary grounds. In Jehlen's view Melville is wrong to uphold "the social order" out of faith in America. Her formulation offers much to disagree with, but at least Jehlen does not confuse her own views with Melville's or distort what takes place in his books.

Her contemporaries do confuse and distort, and the result has been a distinct falling off in the level of literary discourse. To compare criticism about the American classics written before and after 1970 is to mark a loss of the feel for how literature works. Critics now act as if they do not remember how a novel, even though it may include a political brief, remains something very different from a tract. And they write as though ignorant that the primary allegiance of criticism must be to the integrity of the literary object, not to politics.

The literary object's power comes not from its politics but from its unique ways of generating meaning. If contemporary critics were right in assigning political meanings to the American classics, those works would lose their literary status and thereby their usefulness in advancing the critics' political agenda. The works would also lose—have already in part lost—their usefulness as a national literature, which also depends on their retaining literary status.

As things now stand, critical discussion has succeeded in putting America's literature on a plane with America's shortcomings. The critics have achieved a self-fulfilling denigration in which they impose on what they regard as a vulgarly acquisitive America a vulgarized literature. Yet whatever one may think of the nation's political record, its literature is not vulgar except in the uses to which contemporary critics put it.

This is why American literature can still be recovered—and recovered with no less involvement in social, cultural, and even political issues than revisionist critics insist on. Nor will it be necessary in recovering American literature to insist particularly on the socially accommodationist tendencies in Melville and the other authors of the nineteenth-century classics as (disapprovingly) described by Myra Jehlen. For the oppositionism at the heart of their works has been evident from the beginning and cannot help but remain evident. D. H. Lawrence, the first critic to outline American literature as we know it today, observed this oppositionism as long ago as 1923 in his *Studies in Classic American Literature.* "Sensuously, passionately," he wrote of the American authors, "they all attack the old morality." They all wrote, it can be added, from an impulse that was not purely literary but rather, as Perry Miller put it, "in the service of a creed, a career, a philosophy, a disgruntlement or a rage."[11] Recovering American literature does not mean neglecting these extraliterary impulses. But it does mean treating each of them in its literary as well as its political dimensions.

To accomplish this end—and to demonstrate what happens when critics neglect it—I have chosen five fictional works of the nineteenth century: *The Scarlet Letter, Moby-Dick, Billy Budd, Adventures of Huckleberry Finn*, and *The Bostonians.* Most critics would agree that each of these is crucial to the American literary tradition and has also achieved a standing in world literature. The works in question, in common with others I do not discuss, have been distorted so as to satisfy the major tenets of contemporary radical-academic orthodoxy. *The Bostonians* has been rendered into a repudiation of marriage, *Moby-Dick* made a diatribe against capitalist enterprise, *Huckleberry Finn* seen as a repudiation of the Civil War and subsequent racial accommodations, *The Scarlet Letter* regarded as a rejection of society itself, and *Billy Budd* made a rejection of the state (and of the United States in particular). The critics take their case against society and the state yet a step further with Melville's *Typee*. My essay on *Typee*, though it adds to the picture, is set off in an appendix since it deals with a minor work and was previously published in my *The War Against the Intellect*.

Each chapter to follow explores the devolution in critical discussion of one of these American classics. Skewed readings both old and new are assessed, but the point is not to choose among interpretations, much less to introduce interpretations of my own. Instead I have attempted to frame the questions that need to be asked of each work. Recovering American literature, I believe, consists not in attempting to answer these questions, but rather in establishing what they should be. With some agreement about the questions it may be possible to resume the discussion of American books that has been interrupted for nearly twenty-five years.

ONE

The Scarlet Letter: The Heretical Temptation

WHEN *The Scarlet Letter* appeared in 1850 the question immediately arose whether Hawthorne intended his adulterous protagonist, Hester Prynne, to be taken as a saint or a sinner. Sentiment favored Hester as saint, even though the narrator repeatedly calls her guilty. Ignoring the narrator, for nearly a hundred years readers and critics alike sympathized with and defended Hester. Most of them felt that her technical guilt was outweighed by the overwhelming sympathy they had been made to feel for her plight. The young Hester, after all, is shown to have been left alone in the particularly harsh surroundings of a barely settled seventeenth-century Boston. Her husband, incompatibly older than she, is meant to follow her from England, but disappears. Only after he is given up for dead does Hester commit adultery with the young minister of her parish.

At the outset of the book the harsh Puritans of Boston, having discovered that Hester is pregnant, have undertaken to punish her. Ignoring the mitigating circumstances, they impose a humiliating and disproportionate punishment, including the wearing of the scarlet "A." Despite Hawthorne's insistence that Hester is a sinner, therefore, she lives in the reader's imagination as a victim of circumstance, as unfairly treated by society, and as heroic in maintaining her self-respect and allegiance to her love for the minister.

Yet what of her guilt, technical or not? We are outraged at the primitive, public humiliations whereby Hester is made first to stand on a scaffold in the public square and thereafter to wear a scarlet letter over her bosom. But if we put aside these Puritan exaggerations of sin and punishment, what do we make of her adultery, especially after her husband, who turns out to have been captured by Indians, makes his way to Boston? Hawthorne has contrived his plot so that Hester, no matter how much one sympathizes with her, bears at least some responsibility for the events that follow her husband's unexpected return. Once the reader concedes her entanglement in her own fate, he can no longer dismiss the narrator's judgmental commentary on her actions, however much he may dissent from its severity.

To be sure, the commentary seems calculated to provoke its own dismissal. Hester's act of love with the Reverend Dimmesdale is insistently termed a "crime," a "sin," and even "an evil deed." Her refusal to be bowed down by shame at having to wear the letter is seen as shading over into the sin of pride. This pride makes it possible for her to hold up her head while wearing the letter, but the narrator gravely informs the reader that it does not prevent "all the light and graceful foliage of her character" from being "withered up by this red-hot brand." No wonder Anthony Trollope concluded that the same Hawthorne who generated sympathy for Hester must have pronounced severely on her sins "in a spirit of assumed hardness."[1]

Modern readers who feel the same split between sympathy and judgment on Hawthorne's part have sometimes expressed positive resentment at Hester's treatment by the narrator. But Trollope and other readers for the first hundred years of *The Scarlet Letter* did not find Hawthorne's judgment on her incompatible with sympathy. "The reader," Trollope wrote, "is expected to sympathize only with the woman—and will sympathize only with her." Hawthorne's hardness, early readers evidently felt, served to keep before the reader the inescapable fact that Hester had sinned. Just as she never forgets or repudiates her guilt, Trollope in particular seems to be saying, neither can the reader, much as he may wish to. But even though Hester "will bear her doom and acknowledge its justice," the reader, as Trollope sees it, will conclude that "there is no taint of foulness in her love, though there has been deep sin."[2]

Trollope's sympathy, expressed as it is in the unalloyedly sentimental terms of an emotional era, seems to have been positively strengthened by the conviction that Hester is a sinner. In contrast, later readers were often put off by being confronted with her sin. Instead of their sympathy being intensified, they were made uneasy and even resistant to the narrator's point of view. In some ways, as a result, nineteenth-century reflections on *The Scarlet Letter* can be more nuanced than many twentieth-century ones.

For example, in an 1850 review a Massachusetts surgeon, George Loring, explored the disturbing implications of the sympathy one feels toward Hester despite her guilt. One wishes, Loring suggested, not merely to forgive her but also to join her in spirit. Referring to Hawthorne's Puritans, he provokingly asked:

Who has not felt the forbidding aspect of that obtrusive and complacent virtue which never cherishes the thought of forgiveness? And who, that has recognized the deep and holy meaning of the human affections, has not been frozen into demanding a warm-hearted crime as a relief for the cold, false, vulgar, and cowardly asperity which is sometimes called chastity?[3]

In Loring's subtle conception the reader, *frozen* into demanding a warmhearted crime, experiences both resistance to authority and resentment at having been provoked into it.

In the end, nevertheless, Loring went on to pronounce judgment on both Hester and the minister, Arthur Dimmesdale. They have, he writes, a strict responsibility for Pearl, the child they have brought forth. In her waywardness and rebelliousness "this little child typified," Loring severely states, its parents' "self-inflicted contest with and distrust of all mankind." The parents' love, he adds, is "guilty"—"guilty, because, secured as it may have been to them, it drove them violently from the moral centre around which they revolved."[4]

At the outset, then, *The Scarlet Letter* stirred and divided a reader's feelings, on the one hand plunging him into an antinomian spirit of revolt and on the other immersing him in the absolutes of Puritan condemnation. By 1876, though, Loring's acceptance of Hawthorne's strictures was no longer typical. Most readers were squarely on Hester's side. Modern critics went a step further. Not simply do many of them proclaim Hester's right to commit a warmhearted crime, but they add that such a crime's liberating essence renders it a positive good.

Some modern critics carried forward the conviction of most nineteenth-century sentimental readers that Hawthorne was actually in fundamental sympathy with Hester, even to the point of approving the unnamed but presumably heretical thoughts that "visited her" in her "lonesome cottage."[5] But Hawthorne explicitly dismisses Hester's "freedom of speculation," treating it as arising from the disorienting effects of her isolation. He describes her as led by loneliness and desperation to thoughts inappropriate for a woman. And he states that no woman in Hester's melancholy state of mind and spirit can effect the social changes she dreams of. In the end Hester agrees with this view, arriving at "the firm belief" that "in Heaven's own time, a new truth would be revealed, in order to establish the whole relation between man and woman on a surer ground of mutual happiness." Hawthorne expresses a generalized sympathy with Hester's wish for a happier society but firmly rejects her temporary hope that she will be the one to bring about this end.

Soon after the study of American literature became a formal discipline in the 1920s, scholars put together Hawthorne's scattered comments on Hester to show that they added up to a steady indictment. Thereafter it was no longer possible to continue ignoring Hawthorne's criticisms—or to set them aside as not really intended. The so-called romantic reading of *The Scarlet Letter*, in which Hester is unequivocally a heroine, went into a long retreat. At one stage some critics argued that Hawthorne's criticism had not so much to do with Hester's adultery as with her unfortunate agreement to keep the identity of her husband, Roger Chillingworth, hidden from Arthur Dimmesdale. It is true that when she witnesses the results of Chillingworth's worming his way into Dimmesdale's life to take a subtle, psychological revenge, she tells Chillingworth that she can no longer keep his secret and reveals it to Dimmesdale. By then, though, it is too late to save Dimmesdale, and it can be said that Hester has in effect sinned against him (and against their love).

This is certainly a different kind of sin from the formal one of adultery charged by the Puritans. Inasmuch as it violates not society's law but Hester's own ideals, it has been termed a "transcendental" sin in the Emersonian, self-reliant meaning of that word. But the transcendental reading of *The Scarlet Letter*, though persuasive as far as it goes, fails to grapple with the original act of adultery without which Hester's betrayal of Dimmesdale would never have taken place. Nor does the transcendental reading confront Hawthorne's explicit emphasis on that original act.

Writing in 1953, Charles Child Walcutt, who coined the terms "transcendental" and "romantic" to describe approaches to *The Scarlet Letter*, attempted to explain why critics of these persuasions usually tried to avoid Hawthorne's stern judgmentalism. Walcutt suggested that the critics were in effect reflecting Hawthorne's "ambiguity."[6] If romantic readers were wrong to dismiss Hawthorne's judgments, they nevertheless exposed a significant inner tension between those judgments and a warm sympathy. In offering this explanation, Walcutt at one and the same time completed the modern scholarly refutation of romantic readings of *The Scarlet Letter* and left the field open to yet another kind of dismissal of Hawthorne.

It became possible, this time in psychological terms, to regard Hawthorne as not really meaning what he wrote. He was *unconsciously* on Hester's side, and therefore the reader was again free to reject his stern judgments on her. Not only Trollope's assumed hardness formulation lay behind this psychologizing, but also D. H. Lawrence's famous dictum to "trust the tale, not the teller of the tale." In his 1923 essay on Hawthorne, Lawrence urged a distinction between Hawthorne's statements and the actual effect of *The Scarlet Letter*. Like later romantic critics, Lawrence concluded that Hawthorne's deepest attitude toward Hester differed from his explicit statements. But Lawrence believed that Hawthorne harbored not an unconscious sympathy with Hester as much as an unconscious hatred. Trusting the tale, it turned out, meant trusting one's own response to the tale, which could be different from the responses of others.

It remains true that critics ought to be skeptical about comments made by authors after their books have been completed when these contradict the impressions left by their tale. In *The Scarlet Letter*, though, the authorial comments are woven into the story itself; they are an integral part of the tale Lawrence would have us trust. In practical terms, therefore, to set aside Hawthorne's comments on Hester is to trust neither the tale nor the teller of the tale, but rather the interpreter's ability to divine the author's secret thoughts—which ability is contested by other interpreters. Interpretation of *The Scarlet Letter* has to begin with what the author wrote, not his psychology.

In the 1950s few critics continued to celebrate Hester as innocent romantic heroine. One's emotional pull toward her might serve as a starting point for criticism, but Hawthorne's implacable moral judgments could no longer be scanted. Once these judgments were examined closely, moreover, it became apparent that they were not condemnations. To be sure, Henry James, for one, had not been mistaken in sensing "a certain coldness and exclusiveness of treatment" in *The Scarlet Letter*. But if the book's tone felt puritanical in the nineteenth and twentieth centuries, this had to do with how Hawthorne contrived to use Puritanism, not with any allegiance to it on his part. He was, in fact, far harder on the Puritans than on Hester. "The Puritan code" in *The Scarlet*

Letter, Richard Harter Fogle pointed out in 1952, "is arrogant, inflexible, overrighteous; and it is remarked of their magistrates and priests that 'out of the whole human family, it would not have been easy to select the same number of wise and virtuous persons, who should be less capable of sitting in judgment on an erring woman's heart.'"[7] Some critics went so far as to conclude that the critique of Puritanism was the point of *The Scarlet Letter*. But this was to miss Hawthorne's subtle employment of rather than agreement or disagreement with the rigid Puritan morality.

"The Puritans did not invent the seventh commandment," Randall Stewart pointed out in 1958,

> nor were they un-Christian in insisting upon its importance, though an uninformed reader might infer both of these notions from some of the commentaries on *The Scarlet Letter*. The Puritan community in Hawthorne's novel was un-Christian in its unforgiving attitude and behavior—its bigotry and cruelty—but it was not un-Christian in its doctrine.

Of course, Hester's "crime itself is of all crimes the most excusable," as Fogle put it. And the love she shares with Dimmesdale is one "that under different circumstances would have taken a place very high among positive moral values," as Hyatt Waggoner wrote in 1955.[8] Yet all this having been said, these and other critics of the 1950s had come to appreciate Hawthorne's insistence that Hester's adultery was undeniably a crime. That fact remained unaffected by whether one termed the crime a "sin" with the Puritans, or, joining with more enlightened modern sensibilities, preferred to describe it as a "social transgression."

By calling Hester's adultery, which takes place before the action of *The Scarlet Letter*, a sin, Hawthorne was able to extend unaffected sympathy, if not approval, to all her subsequent acts—that is, to everything that occurs in the course of the book. Critics observed that Hawthorne's sympathy, far from being somehow contradictory, or hidden, or unconscious, reflected a subtly conceived artistic strategy. The narrator's insistence on calling Hester a sinner is purposely disturbing yet incontrovertible—unless one is willing to indulge in romantic evasion. Writing in 1952, Darrel Abel called it "a tribute to Hawthorne's art" that romantic readers experienced their allegiance to Hester as a defiance of his intention. For, contrary to their impression, "Hawthorne does feel moral compassion for Hester." She is, Abel added, "more a victim of circumstances than a wilful wrongdoer." But "her role in the story is to demonstrate that persons who engage our moral compassion may nevertheless merit moral censure." Abel admitted: this is "harsh doctrine, but there is no escape from it short of unflinching repudiation of the moral ideas which give man his tragic and lonely dignity."[9]

Richard Harter Fogle was no less firm in insisting that for all the sympathy Hester inspires, "the sin remains real and inescapable." But Fogle was less disapproving than Abel of the romantic reader's identification with her. "Hawthorne permits his reader," Fogle wrote, "...to take his character from his control, to say that Hester Prynne is a great woman unhappily born before her time, or that she is a good woman wronged by her fellow men. But Hawthorne is less confident."[10] Hawthorne's judgment, Fogle and others had made clear, was neither unsympathetic nor rigid. The reader was free to assess the moral issues raised by *The Scarlet Letter* in his own way. No longer, however, could Hawthorne be treated as a prejudiced or unconscious advocate for one or another position on the moral issues.

Three critics of the 1950s warned particularly against the

intellectual self-indulgence in presuming that Hawthorne could be enlisted on the side of the personal liberationist impulse in Hester. "Although we are expected to love and pity Hester," wrote Abel, "we are not invited to condone her fault or to construe it as a virtue." So to construe it, wrote Marius Bewley in 1959, would be to deliver "a disastrously facile moral judgment along 'liberal' lines." One would thereby "reduce the living complexity of art to the comparative vulgarity of a pat resolution." As R. W. B. Lewis summed it up in 1955, "*The Scarlet Letter*, like all very great fiction, is the product of a controlled division of sympathies; and we must avoid the temptation to read it heretically."[11]

For the most part critics did resist the heretical temptation through the 1960s and well into the 1970s. There remained a range of responses to Hester's fallen status, as provided for by Fogle's formulation. But that status was hardly questioned any longer in the older manner of romantic advocacy. Most critics who remained sympathetic both to Hester in general and to her reformist ideas in particular, abandoned the contention that Hawthorne was in secret agreement with her. It was, after all, possible in at least some degree to reconcile Hawthorne's insistence on her guilt with a broader modern morality.

Harold Kaplan, for example, substituted for Hawthorne's purposely exaggerated "sin" and "guilt" of Hester, the word "responsibility." He called attention to the scene in which, shortly before being asked the meaning of the scarlet letter by Pearl, Hester has impulsively removed and thrown aside this badge of shame. In a glade in the forest with Dimmesdale, she lets down her hair and reaffirms her love for him. Pearl, though, is disconcerted by the intimacy between her mother and the minister, and Hester decides to restore herself to a more familiar aspect for the child by putting the letter back on. It is a "dreary," sad moment as Hester also gathers up and replaces her hair under her cap. "Here again was the scarlet misery, glittering on the old spot!" writes Hawthorne, adding that "so it ever is, whether thus typified or no, that an evil deed invests itself with the character of doom."

Surely this is the most stringent hardness assumed by Hawthorne in *The Scarlet Letter*. "Evil deed" shockingly stigmatizes Hester immediately after her single moment of relief and release in the entire seven years chronicled by the book. For Kaplan, though, the replacing of the letter is part of "an insistence on the responsibility of acts, as if to say no relationship is credible unless that responsibility is avowed." From a modern point of view, this is to say, "evil deed" may be translated to mean an act for which Hester must bear responsibility. "Hawthorne insists," adds Kaplan, "that there is nothing gratuitous or inconsequential in a moral event." Indeed, as David Levin pointed out, Hawthorne insisted in *The House of the Seven Gables*, his next book, that "no great mistake, whether acted or endured, in our moral sphere, is ever set right."[12]

In other words, Hester's act most resembles the transgression that sets tragedy in motion. One need not term such an act an evil deed in the Puritan mode: it can be termed an error or a mistake. It can even be the product of a mistake made by someone else—a mistake "endured," as Hawthorne had it in *The House of the Seven Gables*. In the tragic mode that Hawthorne has adopted, though, the deed is treated as morally significant, and its consequences are unflinchingly traced out to their most excruciating ends.

Herein lay the deepest source of the impression that Hawthorne was somehow cold toward Hester. From the tragic perspective he adopted, consequences rather than mitigations had to be his chief concern. Charles Feidelson described Hawthorne's imagination as moving "through the pages in a speculative, inquisitive, experimental mood."[13] The scientist Roger Chillingworth phrases how such an approach applies to Hester when—in his single moment of sympathy in the book—he declares to her: "By thy first step awry thou didst plant the germ of evil but, since that moment, it has all been a dark necessity." In following the logic of that necessity, Hawthorne could not soften the outline of his tale without doing violence to his artistic integrity. Looking back on his work, he appears to have been somewhat put off by its remorselessness, and to have wished that he could have been less Olympianly Sophoclean. In an often-quoted letter written after he had finished the book, Hawthorne wrote, "It is positively a h-ll-fired story, into which I found it impossible to throw any cheering light."

Whether or not they referred to *The Scarlet Letter* as tragic, critics after the 1950s were broadly in agreement that its point lay in the tracing out of "consequences." And they found that Hester's acceptance of the process—her not "denying the negative burden of history," as Charles Feidelson put it—constitutes her "moral achievement."[14] The critics agreed too that Hawthorne's double evocation of both sympathy for and censure of Hester was a calculated effect. The famous ambivalence of his book, therefore, lay within the reader (and the characters), not in Hawthorne.

This did not mean that Hawthorne had a clear, settled view of matters. On the contrary, Darrel Abel argued that it was common for there to be a split between "an author's imaginative capability and his conventional opinions." Taking a similar view of Hawthorne's narrative as both exploratory and multivalent, Austin Warren put it that Hawthorne could have "ambivalent feelings" about Hester and yet still be in artistic control of his materials.[15] However critics might choose to formulate the consensus of the 1950s and 1960s, they were saying that *The Scarlet Letter* is by design calculated to leave unreconciled the conflicting needs of society and the individual.

This formulation was never challenged. Yet starting in the late 1970s it fell almost entirely out of currency, displaced by an altogether different kind of discussion. Some idea of how things changed emerges from the differences between the way one scholarly critic wrote about *The Scarlet Letter* in 1972 and 1985. In 1972 Michael Colacurcio echoed the 1950s consensus through a reference to Hester's famously defiant declaration to Dimmesdale when they are alone together in the forest. "Our love had a consecration of its own," she says to him in defense of what he is committed to treating as their mutual sin. More than any other line in the book, this one had secured generations of romantic readers to Hester's cause, convincing many of them that Hawthorne too was on her side. Colacurcio, though, with perhaps a touch of Hawthorne's hardness, insisted in 1972 that "the world's law validly exists to restrain our disruptive social excesses, however powerful and authentic we feel or 'say' their private consecration to be."[16]

In 1985 Colacurcio turned things the other way round. This time he presented the world's law as neither "valid" nor restraining but as oppressive. It now seemed to him that Hester suffered "subjection to some diffused but scarcely attenuated male authority"—and that this authority was exposed to "Hawthorne's relentless deconstruction [i.e., criticism]."[17] Colacurcio made no mention of having reversed his opinion. Apparently "that was then," as the 1980s expression had it, and this was now. "Then" the world's law could be termed valid; in the academic culture of 1985 such a formulation was all but unthinkable.

Society was now believed to have no such claim on the individual as used to be assumed. Hester, a woman victimized by an uncaring husband and a patriarchal society, is unequivocally to be regarded as good; those who claim otherwise, be they Puritans, modern critics, or Hawthorne himself, are culpably mistaken. The true relationship between society and the individual having become self-evident, no argument in favor of the new view of *The Scarlet Letter* was necessary—not even from a former representative of the old—and hence none was advanced.

Colacurcio, by assuming a "deconstruction" of society by Hawthorne identical to his own view (as of 1985), revived the heretical temptation warned against by R. W. B. Lewis. But in its new form the heresy went further than imagining that Hawthorne held one's own views. It positively demanded that he hold them. For example, the great shift in the discussion of *The Scarlet Letter* of which Colacurcio was a part soon revived all the old justifications of Hester and complaints against Hawthorne. This time, though, except for a lone defense of the 1950s consensus voiced in the late 1970s, no one opposed the heresy. Two or three critics quietly held to the fifties consensus without making an issue of being out of step. Nevertheless, when one of them described *The Scarlet Letter* as opposing "the evanescence of individual self-consciousness" to "the more enduring values of a social order," she was promptly dismissed for making a "staggeringly sanguine pronouncement."[18]

Criticism of the 1980s sometimes gave the appearance of being a discussion containing disagreement as well as agreement. Feminist critics, for example, differed over Hawthorne's attitude toward Hester. Some thought that in his heart he was with them in their unbounded approval of her. Others—the majority—pronounced him unredeemably against her. Feminists critics also differed over the broader question of whether "Hawthorne's treatment of female characters is essentially...protofeminist" or "phallocentric."[19] But these disagreements never really produced a debate. The question of where Hawthorne stood was overshadowed by that of where his readers should stand. Needless to say, feminists entertained no doubts on this point. Their disagreement came down to a friendly divergence over whether or not Hawthorne understood his responsibilities as well as they did.

Because he did not—though a few feminist critics argued that he was unconsciously on their side—his authorial stance now struck them as being more condemnatory than hitherto suspected. They found that Hawthorne treated as nothing but a "crime" the lonely young Hester's adultery with Arthur Dimmesdale, and that he accordingly made her bear "the most responsibility for the outcome of the tale."[20] One critic contended that at the very outset, when Hester is exposed to the Puritan community's stares on the scaffold, she is actually being faulted by Hawthorne for indulging in "self-dramatization." Another critic decided that Hawthorne rejected Hester's political ideas outright, having introduced them only in order to deliver a "subtle and devastating critique of radicalism." As for Hester, she is depicted as behaving "arrogantly," as led astray by "spiritual pride," and as someone who "will not surrender her commitment to her new, desexed intellectual self."

One critic, falling in yet further with Hawthorne's putative condemnations, finds that Hester comes to "falsify" life by quashing her own "impulses" and by allegorizing reality "as rigidly as any Puritan." Another critic has it that she disgracefully "collaborates with Puritan society" by dressing Pearl with allegorical suggestivity. The worst tendencies in Pearl—her "malicious," "perverse" looks—are taken by one critic to be clearly "inherited from her mother," so that Pearl must be understood as "a shadowy reflection of evil." And finally, still another critic has it that Hester "abuses or represses" her better qualities so as to render herself a "hypocrite" and a "liar."[21]

The so-called orthodox critics of the 1950s and 1960s, at the height of their zeal to refute the approval of Hester characteristic of romantic readings, never thought that Hawthorne made Hester half so guilty as critics of the 1980s supposed. Like revolutionaries whose savage descriptions of the Old Regime correspond chiefly to the reality that they themselves eventually bring into existence, critics of the 1980s went from accusing Hawthorne of treating Hester puritanically, to in effect doing so themselves. Settling the issue of *The Scarlet Letter*'s studied ambivalence entirely in favor of Hester, but dissatisfied by Hawthorne's failure to do so, they were led to imagine that he had rendered her nearly monstrous. Hawthorne's Puritans never went so far.

It naturally followed that the savage treatment of Hester supposedly administered by Hawthorne called for an explanation. The old notion that he was psychologically divided about Hester was therefore given a new, as it were pathological, twist. He was now seen to have suffered from a "tortured ambivalence." His treatment of Hester reflected "his own dilemma" and was actually "an attempt to work out his ambiguity toward himself." The source of Hawthorne's confusion was "his own sublimated sexuality." One critic was able specifically to trace his "repressed authorial anxieties" to his "sublimated incest wishes" for his mother.[22] In the past, psychological speculation tended to conclude that Hawthorne's double perspective lent *The Scarlet Letter* its peculiar power. Now a disabling inner dividedness was seen as the source of the book's failure.

Some critics traced the dividedness to Hawthorne's fear of social disapproval if he were to reveal his (presumed) attraction to Hester's heterodoxy. He was, we are told, "partly aware" of this fear and even had a "sense" that his "creative life" depended on identifying with Hester. Yet he could not let himself support her. And so, to escape from his attraction he devised a narrator whose remarks would "drain some of the force from Hester's passionate nature" and "weaken or... qualify the impact" of her dangerous thoughts. The critics proceeded to expose this narrator, though they were obviously "partly aware" that in so doing they were attacking Hawthorne himself. The "narrator," they concluded, criticizes Hester out of "fear of disapproval" should he do otherwise. Hester is "deeply threatening" to the narrator, and her declaration that "our love had a consecration of its own" positively "shocks" him. (This according to the Michael Colacurcio of 1985; in 1972 he had it that "the narrator... feels—with Hester—that [she] had fulfilled her passionate self for the first time in her life.")

Not all critics try to separate the narrator from Hawthorne, though: some accuse him directly of a "failure of courage."[23] In the 1980s critical disagreement over *The Scarlet Letter* was restricted to the question of whether Hawthorne's "failure" should be attributed to psychological need, to a need to meet the demands of the marketplace (i.e., capitalism was the culprit), to the effects of the contemporary women's movement, or to the revolutions of 1848 in Europe (yet another putative source of fright). But all agreed that he should have done otherwise than he did: he should have been more "subversive." Decidedly, *The Scarlet Letter* should not breathe a "strong [politically] reactionary spirit" as it does, nor end "with affirmation of the state and its representatives." It is unfortunate that Hawthorne's "ideological limitations" reflect "the complicity of his art with those programs that promote domination and subjection in society."[24]

The notorious ambiguity of *The Scarlet Letter* was now solved. Rather than being an authorial technique, this ambiguity reflects a "general linguistic imprecision," or else "a confusing ambivalence" thanks to which Hawthorne "fails" the reader. He most certainly does fail a certain kind of reader by not championing Hester, and speaking for that reader numerous critics now expressed disappointment and resentment by at once devaluing *The Scarlet Letter* and attacking Hawthorne. Once again the narrator was blamed at first, then Hawthorne as well. To the charge that the narrator is psychologically damaged was now added the charge that he is hopelessly inconsistent and incompetent at telling a story. The "intellectually incoherent" narrator's criticisms of Hester are "fitful cavils." He displays "contradictions in his voice as well as his story" and incompetently "impedes...the progress of the novel." His errors range from "unwittingly" contradicting himself in an "unconscionable" manner to resorting to "punitive plotting."[25]

The narrator's ambivalence serves to disguise "his fearful cruelty of heart," which he presumably shares with Hawthorne even as he resembles him in being "a Dimmesdale who doesn't quite know he is a Chillingworth." Hawthorne's "ideological limitations," and his "abdication" of the individualist message the book should have conveyed, were a succumbing "to life defined by the scaffold" (or, as another critic put it, like "a fatalistic alliance with the prison's 'darkening close'"). In other words, contrary to what the critics of the 1950s and 1960s thought, Hawthorne was not actually in control of his materials. How could he possibly be in control given his disgraceful attitudes?[26]

In the course of dismissing Hawthorne's art, the critics grew artless. In an almost childlike fashion some of them began to treat not only the narrator but also Hawthorne's characters as though they were real. The phrase "punitive plotting," for example, charged Hawthorne with mistreating a Hester in effect conceived of as a real person. The same confusion of realms governed another critic's accusations: that Hawthorne is guilty toward Hester for "stripping her of her capacity to act," after which he "condemns her to silence" (presumably on feminist-political issues). And confusion lurked in a third critic's dismissal of Hawthorne's narrative itself. "He *claims*," wrote this critic resentfully, "that 'all the light and graceful foliage of her character had been withered up' by the scarlet letter" (italics added).[27] The critic feels she knows better—knows and loves the real Hester better than Hawthorne. As one critic well described the resentful 1980s reaction to *The Scarlet Letter* (which he shared), we "construct" an ideal Hester "and then must confront Hawthorne's failure to actualize her in his text."[28]

Obsessed with the radical politics they imagine Hester to share, contemporary critics limit themselves to the question of whether Hawthorne is or is not politically correct. Not really attempting either to inquire into or interpret *The Scarlet Letter*, but rather ideologically interrogating it, they appear unable to think in any but the unliterary language of either/or. Feminist critics ask themselves whether Hawthorne is a protofeminist or a misogynist. But having jettisoned literary values, they have no way of disputing even this crude question with one another. Other critics ask whether Hawthorne wrote from a conservative or progressive point of view, but employ discriminations too blunt to settle the question. For example, one of them quotes Hawthorne's college letter to his mother in which he humorously reported on his drinking and gambling at cards (for which he was fined several times). The critic then takes this youthful naughtiness as evidence that the later Hawthorne was on the correct political side. "Those critics who find in *The Scarlet Letter* more approval than disapproval for the deeply conservative ways of seventeenth-century Puritan society," he writes, "might do well to read this frank communication between a twenty-year-old Hawthorne and his mother."[29] Literature having been reduced to politics, the critic's argument has here become a caricature of literary inquiry.

Hawthorne's creation requires an entirely different kind of imaginative exercise from what it received in the 1980s. Little insight is needed to indulge oneself in naturally arising sympathy for and support of Hester. But something of an imaginative effort is needed to appreciate the limitations of such a response. Hawthorne indicated the kind of spirit he required in his reader by making the scarlet letter ambiguous. The Puritans themselves, years after they affix the crude, reductive "A" for adultery to Hester's bosom, begin to see it differently. They informally come to invest it with the meaning "able," in recognition of Hester's selfless devotion to the ill and the poor. This alteration of meaning has its analogue in the tendency of readers to soften "adultery," with its harsh overtones, to "forgivable transgression," or "justified passion," or "true love," or even "admirable."

The reader who chooses the last of these is mistaken if he fancies himself in defiance of Hawthorne, whose ambiguity about the meaning of the letter virtually dictates a range of responses to it—among readers as among the Puritans. No theory of authorial confusion or hidden psychological strains or incompetence is needed to account for the reader's feeling that in his own view of Hester's situation he is at odds with others. Indeed, to regard Hester's badge of shame in any way other than that originally intended by Hawthorne's Puritan magistrates is to begin asserting alternate moral and social values—and to discover that one's contemporaries do not precisely share these values.

Clearly it is essential to Hawthorne's design that the claims of society should initially be put in a bad light by Puritan absolutism, with its violations of the individual in both body and spirit. Critics are comfortable with modern works of literature that make us see the necessity of upholding the prerogatives of even the most undeserving and distasteful individual, but the same critics are distinctly uncomfortable with the prerogatives Hawthorne makes us consider: those of a distasteful society. In doing so, Hawthorne set his work apart from the novels of his contemporaries in which Puritan heroines struggled under the weight of their society's oppressions. These intrepid dissenters invariably led society forward to greater freedom and happiness for the individual. Hawthorne, in contrast, created a heroine out of a tragic sense of the fate that can lie in store for the dissenter.[30]

This seems to be the point intended by Mrs. Hawthorne when she described *The Scarlet Letter* to her sister in a letter written after listening to her husband read the just-completed manuscript. "It is most powerful," she wrote, "& contains a moral as terrific & stunning as a thunderbolt. It shows that the Law cannot be broken."[31] Significantly, Sophia Hawthorne says nothing of the protagonist who breaks the law. Grasping the larger point, she does not speak of Hester's guilt or innocence. Nor does she refer to breaking the law as immoral or moral. The moral in the sense of what has been demonstrated is the main thing, and this moral is that "the Law cannot be broken" with impunity. As in a tragic play, we are reminded that any serious violation of law, no matter how defensible or excusable in itself, may have dread consequences.

Richard Chase commented on the same inevitability when he pointed out that Hester's fate was at once peculiar to Puritan society and universal: the result "not of man's living in sin but of his living in a Puritan society, and thereby, to some extent in *any* society." Every society, this is to say, regards certain acts as transgressions, and punishes them. Hawthorne is therefore judging neither Hester's sins in particular nor Puritan society in general, but rather exploring what happens when the norms of society are violated. His subject is, to quote Chase again, "the moral and psychological results of sin—the isolation and morbidity, the distortion and thwarting of the emotional life."[32]

It is all too easy to dismiss as philosophically irrelevant *The Scarlet Letter*'s Puritans and their utterly punitive attitude toward adultery. Yet even at the end of the twentieth century there remains a modern analogy with the values of a Puritan society in our continued if diminished disapproval of adultery. Nor would *The Scarlet Letter* be rendered obsolete if this analogy should disappear because adultery ceased being regarded as a violation. The reader would then be obliged to search for another analogy. And that analogy, like adultery itself, would have to convey the sense in which Hawthorne's Puritans are fundamentally right when they intolerantly and perversely associate Hester's sin of adultery with all other sin—with the original sin in the garden as well as with murder. They are right, the analogy would need to remind us, because all violations of norms are linked. This is why parents punish children for small offenses.

No more would the link between past and present be broken if one searched for one's analogy in a contemporary oppressive society where the norms themselves are perverted. So much the better, in fact, for certifying the timelessness of *The Scarlet Letter* if one could find an *endured* wrong to match Hawthorne's *House of Seven Gables* statement that "no great mistake, whether acted or endured, in our moral sphere, is ever set right." For example, a rough analogue to Hester's transgression and punishment can be imagined in the former Soviet Union. A private businessman there, let us say, is arrested and punished for the crime of "speculation"— earning money privately in a manner that would be looked on in the West as "able" or admirable. The victim might well feel innocent yet at the same time suffer from guilt at violating the socialist norm which all around him is supported with a piety as intense as Puritan righteousness. (There would be those even in the West—conceivably among the champions of Hester Prynne—who would agree with the state that individualist "speculation" was evil.)

Only after long reflection would the Soviet victim come to regard his act as defensible, and conclude that society, not he, required reformation. The Russian Hawthorne telling this tale would want to concentrate not on his Hester's innocence but on the train of unhappy results following from committing the crime of speculation. At some point this Hawthorne might have his character somehow manage to come to America and there find sympathy for his pain and suffering. After a time, though, his denunciations of the Soviet Union, with which all agree, might well come to seem obtrusive. This victim would prove to be one of those whose personality has been "withered" by his martyrdom. In the end he could, like Hester after her sojourn in England, return to his country, now grown sympathetic to his point of view. Yet once there he would sense that the effects on him of his fate have rendered him ineligible to be the one who will lead his fellows to a better dispensation, and he puts his faith in a more generalized, spiritual renewal of society.

The point of such a tale would not be criticism of the defunct communist system. Nor would the reader be called upon merely to sympathize with its victim and endorse his ideas. Instead the reader would be expected to reflect on the ways that suffering can injure the spirit even as it focuses the mind, and on the ways in which we are ineluctably tied to society irrespective of its political and ideological arrangements. Yet reflections such as these were not prompted in critics of the 1980s when they read *The Scarlet Letter*. Instead they fixed their attention exclusively on the sins of the book's oppressive society and on the case to be made for its victim.

They thereby reduced to the single dimension of ideology a book whose central concern is precisely with the warping effects of ideology. The question of which side is right in the struggle between the punitive ideology of the Puritans and Hester's resistance to it in the name of natural impulse and personal freedom is not meant to be adjudicated. The Puritans are not wrong to regard any violation of law as a potential threat to social order. Nor is Hester wrong to maintain personal dignity in the face of her denigrating punishment—as her growth in character and intellect sufficiently confirms. Yet as Hawthorne shows, the manner in which each ideology is held can prove injurious to the spirit.

Certainly the rigidly committed, narrowly conceived manner in which critics of the 1980s championed Hester and individual rights proved injurious to literature. The critics delivered precisely the "disastrously facile moral judgement along 'liberal' lines" that Marius Bewley had warned would be "fatal to criticism." Putting ideology before literary value, these critics luridly represented *The Scarlet Letter* as a puritanical assault on Hester Prynne, patronized Hawthorne, and ultimately denounced and dismissed his book as written. Thanks to their fanatical allegiance to the otherwise admirable ideal of individual freedom, they emptied a literary work of its literary value. This left them with nothing better to contemplate than their own ideological preconceptions.

T W O

Moby-Dick:
Cutting a Classic Down
to Ideological Size

THAT *Moby-Dick* is an adventure story with a meaning was as apparent to reviewers in 1851 as to the academics who have studied it from a spectrum of points of view in the course of the twentieth century. Melville, as scholarship has amply shown, was a lifelong metaphysical questioner and quester. And both Captain Ahab and his crew member/narrator, Ishmael, are interested in the particular whale, Moby Dick, as much for his meaning as for his actuality. On the other hand, Melville distrusted settled answers to the profound questions of life. It would be a mistake, he has Ishmael write, to regard *Moby-Dick* as "a hideous, intolerable allegory."

The remark is typical of the book's humorously riddling complexity. The reader addressed is one who may mistakenly regard the descriptions of whaling in general and the particular whale Moby Dick as fantastic. "So ignorant are most landsmen of some of the plainest and most palpable wonders of the world," sententiously explains Ishmael, "that without some hints touching the plain facts, historical and otherwise, of the fishery, they might scout at *Moby-Dick* as a monstrous fable, or still worse and more detestable, a hideous and intolerable allegory." Clearly comic here are Ishmael's standard tall-tale protestation that *Moby-Dick* is no tall tale, and his tongue-in-cheek explanation that its hundreds of pages of cetology—the science of whales—had to be inserted strictly in order to set landsmen straight. When he himself soon proceeds to moralize and allegorize the cetological details, the warning against allegory is given yet another comic turn. One is left with the conclusion that *Moby-Dick* is most certainly allegorical, yet that attempts to nail down its meanings are not likely to succeed.

By "allegory" Melville no doubt meant first of all religious allegory. And manifestly Ahab's refusal to accept the loss of his leg to Moby Dick as a random event stems from the question of whether the universe is directed by the Christian god or some other principle (or nonprinciple). The action of *Moby-Dick* is driven by this religious question and by the iconoclasm with which Ahab is determined to answer it. At the same time Ahab's determination is a cultural phenomenon. His lonely lucubrations on his wound are directly linked to the peculiarly American Calvinist tradition of obsessive speculation and searching for meaning.

Ahab's search thereby helps portray an entire people in accordance with Melville's evident purpose to write an American epic. This purpose is signaled by numerous extended similes in the manner of the *Iliad* and the *Aeneid*, many of which have to do with the American landscape and American domestic ways. The multinational crew of Ahab's ship, the *Pequod*, furthermore, represents the American mixture of peoples. And Melville treats these peoples in epic fashion in his famous chapters on "Knights and Squires." Here he celebrates the "kingly commons"—the lowborn but heroic crew of the whaling ship—as the equals of any aristocratic, heroic figures sung by previous epic authors.

On the other hand Ahab is an authoritarian. As Starbuck exclaims, "He would be a democrat to all above; look how he lords it over all below!" This is to say that if Ahab's challenge to the heavens expresses a democratic/religious heritage, his control over and humiliations of the common people as represented by the crew are decidedly antidemocratic. Obviously Melville means to bring to mind the ancient wisdom that democracy is the form most susceptible to the demagogic leader. In this context, as critics have long noted, *Moby-Dick* may be said to have broadly social and political meaning. In the 1980s, though, this meaning came to be reduced to precisely the settled answers of allegory that Melville had warned against. To understand how this came about, it is necessary to go back to the formative period of American academic criticism.

In 1941, in *American Renaissance*, F. O. Matthiessen described the famous "kingly commons" peroration in *Moby-Dick* as a "fusion of Christianity and democracy." Here and elsewhere Melville located the source of the divine spirit of equality among men in the spiritual equality offered by Christianity. This meant that, like much else in *Moby-Dick*, the democratic element was spiritual before it was political. The nature of the democratic element was further complicated by its inherent imperfections. From the beginning of his writing career, as Matthiessen showed, Melville "did not sentimentalize the sailor." On the contrary, in the scene of "needless cruelty" to a dying whale on the part of Flask, the third mate, Melville took a harshly critical view of the common man. (Matthiessen regarded Flask's cruelty as representative not of the officer class but of common humanity.) "Though whaling is necessary to civilization," Matthiessen concluded, "still this crew may deserve something of the retribution that overtakes it." Finally, though it was important to assess Melville's attitudes toward social class, Matthiessen concluded that, after all, "Melville's tragedies are more concerned with spiritual and metaphysical issues even than with the economic and social."[1]

In 1951 Henry Nash Smith explored "The Image of Society in *Moby-Dick*" to determine Melville's social-political point of view or tendency. Smith found, somewhat incidentally, that Ahab is "endowed with menacing and irresistible force through being associated with the machines of the Industrial Revolution." Evidently with Matthiessen in mind, Smith observed that "this imagery has seemed to support the interpretation of Ahab as an embodiment of the inhuman will-to-power which Melville discerned in developing American capitalism. Yet I do not think that the industrial imagery, taken as a whole, provides, or was meant to provide, a coherent image of American society."[2] Matthiessen, alluding to the so-called robber barons of American industry, had suggested that Ahab's "career is prophetic of many others in the history of later nineteenth-century America." But if Melville had been "prophetic" of what was to come, Matthiessen added, it was "without deliberately intending it."[3]

In addition, Matthiessen wrote of Melville that even where he confronted nascent industrial capitalism directly, his "main concern was not with studying the factory system, but with human suffering wherever he found it."[4] Matthiessen and Smith therefore agreed that Melville's social and political attitudes were secondary. But they differed in their estimates of these attitudes. What Matthiessen took as prophetic of capitalist excesses struck Smith as vague and intellectually dubious. Smith wrote, for example, that Melville delivered a "radical accusation of unjust force" against governments in the famous "Fast-Fish, Loose-Fish" chapter. (Loose-Fish are slain whales that have drifted to where they can be seized by anyone.) Here Melville had philosophized on other seizures of unsecured property such as that of the Mexican territory taken by the United States, and the seizure of persons into slavery. Smith was hard on the passage, in which, he charged,

> the denial of any moral basis for political institutions is finally carried to the utmost extremity: "What are the Rights of Man and the Liberties of the World but Loose-Fish? What all men's minds and opinions but Loose-Fish?" I do not see how [the passage] can be described as anything except philosophical anarchy, with the strong overtones of primitivism that philosophical anarchy usually has.[5]

Smith made two points about the social and political in *Moby-Dick*. First, though the "democratic dignity" celebrated in the "Knights and Squires" chapter "is the central affirmation of the novel," it is on the other hand "not primarily a social value at all. The democracy which Melville has in mind is not a political system or even a social system. It is independent of institutions." Richard Chase, among others, would make the same point in the course of the 1950s. Second, Smith judged Melville's social and political ideas to be not only philosophically irresponsible but also confused. For example, the alternative to Ahab's destructive nihilism is Ishmael's discovery of brotherhood. This discovery is affirmed through Ishmael's surviving the wreck of the *Pequod*, his miraculous immunity from the sharks as he floats in the sea, and his almost equally miraculous delivery by the ship *Rachel*.

But Smith observes that "in a universe without God [such as one finds in *Moby-Dick*], such a miracle is hard to account for." Nor, in Smith's opinion, is Ishmael's discovery of brotherhood "sufficiently specified." Instead, "at the end of the book, we are convinced it has occurred, but we are not fully able to say how or why."[6]

Smith's and Matthiessen's readings are admirable for their willingness to question the literary status of Melville's fervid declarations of egalitarianism as well as his recurrent gestures toward a radical criticism of society. After all, Matthiessen was a political radical dedicated to egalitarianism, and Smith apparently a left-leaning liberal. Matthiessen, furthermore, had declared the common element among the writers discussed in his *American Renaissance* to be "their devotion to the possibilities of democracy."[7] Yet Matthiessen, Smith, and most other critics through the 1950s refused to make too much of Melville's explicit devotion to these possibilities. Regarding those passages in *Moby-Dick* where social criticism or preaching the democratic doctrine became undeniably prominent, Smith in particular emphasized Melville's literary failure to integrate them coherently.

Beginning in the 1960s the primacy of literary judgment exemplified by Matthiessen and Smith was to suffer an erosion and then a reversal. The social and political element in *Moby-Dick* was first deemed more extensive, then more central, then more coherent than critics through the 1950s had maintained. Eventually the social and political were deemed worthy to stand on their own, divorced from the metaphysical element of the book. Critics now arrived at a broad agreement that the social and political element was far more politically radical than had been thought. Not only this, but they agreed that the fundamental meaning of *Moby-Dick* was political.

The groundwork for cutting *Moby-Dick* down to political size was laid by two highly informative but potentially misleading scholarly articles that appeared at the turn of the 1960s. In these, Charles Foster and Alan Heimert uncovered a rich web of allusion by Melville to the political controversies of his day. Charles Foster found echoes from antislavery sermons of the 1840s in Father Mapple's sermon on Jonah early in the book. Alan Heimert demonstrated that political speeches in the 1840s frequently employed the ship-of-state metaphor implicit in *Moby-Dick* to warn against the Mexican War and the threat of civil war over slavery. The question raised by both articles was how and to what extent Melville's use of contemporary rhetoric indicated a taking of political positions in *Moby-Dick*.

Foster theorized that the events of the early 1850s, particularly the Compromise of 1850 (permitting the extension of slavery into some of the territories being settled in the West), had turned a politically cautious Melville into a fierce opponent of slavery. As a result, "in the spring and summer of 1851," with "great energy and skill" he inserted into his nearly complete manuscript "radical passages and sometimes chapters" that amounted to a buried, nearly imperceptible "antislavery fable." The fable had gone undetected because "with almost equal energy and skill" Melville had "covered his tracks, withdrawing into ambiguities and symbols difficult even yet to decipher."[8]

For Alan Heimert, *Moby-Dick* particularly reflected contemporary rhetoric critical of American expansionism. His findings overlapped with Foster's insofar as opposition to territorial expansion had been based on objections to the extension of slavery. If "as one suspects," Heimert agreed with Foster, Melville invites the reader "to approach *Moby-Dick* as something of a political 'fable,'" then Ishmael's point of view has been clearly identified with the 'Barnburners,' or 'Free Soilers,' as their opposition to the extension of slavery led them to be called."[9] But if Melville flirted with outright abolitionism, Heimert continues, he ended, contrary to Foster's analysis, as its critic.

Melville supported the Compromise of 1850, as abolitionists decidedly did not, and in the end rested in "the democratic faith" that the slavery issue would yet be solved peacefully. Heimert did insist that Melville incorporated in *Moby-Dick* some of the strains of expansion, slavery, and secession. And that both before and after *Moby-Dick*, "he continued to question the imperialist ambitions of American Democracy."[10] But Heimert also found that Melville's anti-expansionism reflected not radicalism but the current Whig, prudential dislike of adventurism. The same dislike, even though Melville "detested" slavery, kept him firmly opposed to antislavery extremism.

Heimert and Foster's rival interpretations provided an object lesson in the risks of attempting to assign a fixed political meaning to *Moby-Dick*. But the two critics did uncover numerous contemporary references to highly charged public issues. Once one recognizes these as a contemporary reader would have, a good deal of bite is added to the famous evocations of democratic equality. In one of its moods at least, *Moby-Dick* does indeed display a "visceral democracy" (Heimert), or even a "commitment to radical democracy" (Foster).[11] But to say this is still not to impose any specific political allegory on *Moby-Dick*.

Soon after Foster and Heimert's essays appeared in the early 1960s, there took place a revival of 1930s-style interest in Matthiessen's "possibilities of democracy." In the second radical decade of the twentieth century, though, the emphasis shifted from celebration of these possibilities to condemnation of the American historical record. The critic Leo Marx showed the way by seizing on a single element in his teacher Henry Nash Smith's essay on *Moby-Dick*: the malevolent images of machines. By omitting both Smith's literary analysis of these images and his contention that they never added up to a coherent image of American society, Marx was able to politicize them.

Smith had put it that Melville chiefly exploited "the ominous character of the machine . . . to express Ahab's inhuman determination to use the crew of the *Pequod* as mere tools." Leo Marx now asserted that the point of the machine comparisons was not so much to expose Ahab's inhumanity as to illustrate that, as Karl Marx also believed, "the Age of Machinery transforms men into objects."[12] Following Leo Marx, other critics of the 1960s, without necessarily bringing Karl Marx into the picture, began to isolate Matthiessen's "economic and social" element.

Responding to the heightened social consciousness of the decade, critics gradually assumed the coherent social picture of America said by Smith not to exist. For a time they were apologetic. Milton Stern, for example, in his 1969 essay "*Moby-Dick*, Millenial Attitudes, and Politics," called his own isolating of "the political level of the book" a "distortion." But his distortion actually had to do less with isolating than with moralizing politics. He emphasized in the traditional way the temperamental and metaphysical contrast between Ahab and Ishmael. With justice he described Ahab's manipulation of the crew as dictatorial, and Ishmael's contrasting "marriage to the world of actual men" as an "accommodating democracy."[13] This much fell squarely in the tradition of Matthiessen's treating Ishmael as a representative of democratic brotherhood.

Where Stern went astray was in his treatment of Ahab's

"totalitarian" tendency. This term too went back respectably to Matthiessen, for whom the totalitarian dictators of the 1930s provided a contemporary angle on Ahab. Leo Marx, though, had once again escalated the insight, asserting that "Melville anticipates the twentieth century's discovery that prudential, rationalistic cultures are peculiarly vulnerable to leaders of mad purpose."[14] In the 1960s, of course, parallels between American presidents and the totalitarian Hitler—though not often the totalitarian Stalin—became the common coin of political radicalism. Taking up the rhetoric of the day along with Leo Marx, Stern referred to the congressional resolution that permitted President Lyndon Johnson to send troops to Vietnam. The scene in which Ahab swears the crew to the pursuit of *Moby-Dick* became for Stern a "Gulf of Tonkin mandate," that is, a deception to make possible an illegal aggression. The American president's actions regarding Vietnam were, in Stern's view, Hitlerian, totalitarian manipulations like Ahab's. He therefore concluded, with a touch of melodrama of his own, that such political actions were precisely what Melville had warned against: "The rhetoric and the causes of the führers and commissars and 'democratic' demagogues will kill you, [Melville] says to the millions of the peopled earth."[15]

Stern would have been on surer ground if he had had in mind an already accomplished abuse of power by an American demagogue. As it stood, his argument that Melville accurately prophesied such an abuse depended on his personal worries of the moment about the ambitions of Lyndon Johnson—a man actually about to surrender the presidency. That Ahab evokes fears of demagogy is undeniable. But so is the historical record, in which eccentrics of his stripe have always remained marginal in America. Their existence therefore not only points up some of the darker impulses in the democracy, as the critics have it, but also the immunity rather than susceptibility of "rationalistic cultures" to totalitarians. More characteristic of such cultures, it develops, has it been to produce grave warnings against totalitarianism by critics like Stern and Marx. After the 1960s, when the warnings might have been expected to abate, the critics' fears instead increased, until their growing preoccupations with American evil came to dominate critical writing on *Moby-Dick*.

Recently, a University of Kansas professor traced this escalation in the course of an essay on how current events and changing academic ideologies influenced her teaching. Elizabeth Schultz's remarkably frank account of how she presented *Moby-Dick* to students over the years begins in 1967. She recalls that at that time she emphasized Ishmael's pregnant observation that it is impossible to see the whale in its entirety. As she analyzed it, this observation could be interpreted as "Ishmael's attempt to communicate to us, to convince us that life is good though we cannot know it absolutely, though we can only continue to try to know it. It is a commitment to process rather than to progress."[16]

In 1967 this interpretation represented a rather unpolitical version of Matthiessen's opposition between Ahab's moral absolutism and Ishmael's genial acceptance of uncertainty. Schultz, though, appears to be investing her recollection of how she taught with a dose of 1980s moralism when she represents Ishmael as attempting to "communicate to us." It seems more likely that she adopted the objective teaching manner of the day and restricted herself to presenting Ishmael's compromise with life as his own rather than as a vulgar attempt to proselytize. But she has otherwise captured the academic approach to *Moby-Dick* that prevailed through the 1960s.

"In the spring of 1971," Schultz continues her account,

"America is in conflict in Viet Nam, and in conflict with itself.... At the University of Kansas, the Union has burned; the military science building and the computer science center have been bombed... new courses and new degrees are being created—they must be 'relevant.'" This summary is in no way meant to be either ironic or critical of the way events intruded on college instruction. On the contrary, promptly enough, in Schultz's own class, "Melville and *Moby-Dick* resounded with 'relevancy.'" For her the book was transformed: "Before this class in 1971, I'd not realized how fully *Moby-Dick* resonates with the strengths and weaknesses of our culture." It now emerged that "both Ahab and Ishmael are rebels," and that they share "anti-authoritarianism."[17]

In the remaining account of 1971 that follows, Schultz, very much in the spirit of the period, represents her interpretation as coming from the students. Presumably they just happen to have "perceived" in their assigned readings the basis for the radical politicizations then being introduced into classrooms under the guise of literary analysis. But it is obvious that her reference to the "extinct" Pequot Indians after whom Melville's whaleship is named can hardly have come from the students. Had any of them knowledge of this New England tribe from their history books, it would not have included the accusation, just then being leveled by radical revisionist historians, that the Puritans exterminated the Pequots. (The accusation was eventually refuted.)[18]

In Professor Schultz's account the students of 1971 "perceived quite rightly" that

Ahab's ship, the *Pequod*, was, among other things, a ship of state and a factory ship, that is, a representation of the democratic system, with its industrial underpinnings. They saw that Melville had mixed feelings about both democracy and capitalism, that indeed he regarded both America's political and economic system with equal eye. Seeing their strengths, he also saw them veering toward imperialism. Given my students' awareness of racial tensions in and military aggression by the United States in 1971, they appreciated Melville's irony in naming his ship after an extinct tribe of Massachusetts Indians. They applauded Ishmael's antipathy toward whiteness as a color associated with imperialism, and they deprecated Stubb's bullying attitude toward the black cook and the black cabin boy.

The capitalistic system, imperialism, race...these were what *Moby-Dick* was supposed to be about as of 1971—along with "exploitation of natural resources" (mentioned a bit further on in Schultz's account).

"Through the seventies and into the eighties," Professor Schultz continues her account, certain feelings—strictly on the students' parts, of course—entered her classroom. The sinking of the *Pequod* now suggested a prophecy of nuclear "Armageddon." By 1988, the date of Professor Schultz's article, *Moby-Dick* conveyed the political homily that "it remains possible for us as individuals to choose to work to curtail" the production of nuclear weapons. And "personally, *Moby-Dick* convinces me," adds Professor Schultz, "to work to prevent ecological, economic, or political catastrophe." Nor is this all. For "I have also been teaching women's literature courses," writes Professor Schultz. *Moby-Dick*, it now develops, reflects "our patriarchal society." And Ahab's "single-minded vision," as it turns out, "is anti-feminist."[19]

The sources of Professor Schultz's conversion in the spring of 1971 are traced further back by Carolyn Karcher in her *Shadow Over the Promised Land: Slavery, Race and Violence in*

Melville's America (1980). She "discovered a side of Melville I had always overlooked," she reports, thanks to "the Civil Rights and anti–Vietnam War movements." They made her realize that in the course of his career Melville "had written impassioned indictments of American and European imperialism... slavery... pauperism and mistreatment of emigrants ... floggings and militarism... the betrayal of American Revolutionary ideals... the complacency of the rich and the exploitation of the working class."

Melville had also—though this insight appears to derive from somewhat later than the civil rights and anti–Vietnam War periods—"paid eloquent homage to the courageous endurance of a woman victimized by the greed and lust of men."[20]

Karcher and Schultz establish that by 1971 the politicization of *Moby-Dick* that would be typical of criticism in the 1980s was virtually complete. All that remained was to add homosexuals and American Indians to the ranks of the exploited, to add a note of bitterness to that of outrage, and to claim exclusivity for the politicized view. By 1983 Robert Milder could observe (in the annual, *American Literary Scholarship*) that "by chance or not, all of the year's longer writings dealt in one way or another with Melville and politics."[21] It was not necessary to specify that "politics" here referred to the imposition on *Moby-Dick* of contemporary political issues deemed important to academics on the left.

Despite the exaggerations produced by the politicizing of *Moby-Dick*, it is not wrong to say that Melville had American capitalism much in mind as he wrote. That the voyage of the *Pequod* is a capitalist venture cannot be doubted. Nor is it possible to miss the implication that Ahab is a captain of industry, inasmuch as he directs a full-scale factory ship. For his American epic Melville appropriately chose a characteristically American, entrepreneurial, industrial undertaking for the central action. Richard Chase spoke for most critics of the 1950s when he termed Ahab an "epic transmutation of the free enterpriser."[22]

Yet if in *Moby-Dick* "the myth is capitalism," as Chase put it, capitalism never became an analytic category for Melville.[23] Ahab is a heroic figure who happens to be cast in a capitalist mode. He would have been a heroic warrior for an epic of archaic Greece, or a slayer of dragons rather than whales for an epic of the Anglo-Saxons, or a sea explorer instead of a hunter for an epic of Renaissance Portugal (to name three periods in which epics that influenced Melville were created).[24]

To be sure, some critics have always given greater weight than others to the capitalist-American element. But as Philip Gleason observed in 1963, before that date "no one, except perhaps an occasional Marxist," had given *Moby-Dick* an "out and out political interpretation." Before the 1960s, moreover, not even Marxists claimed that capitalism told the whole story. The Marxist James B. Hall, for example, in "*Moby-Dick*: Parable of a Dying System" (1950), predictably treated Ahab as driven "by the spirit of free enterprise" and as representing industrialism "in the very image of himself: ruthless, cunning, and fatal." But Hall concluded that "the implications of the economic aspects—*Moby-Dick* as Industrial Saga—do not, it seems to me, present the most relevant meaning of the book."[25]

Despite this disclaimer, after the 1960s Hall's kind of Marxist anticapitalism came to be accepted without reservations. In 1964, the year following Philip Gleason's relegation of the political interpretation to the occasional Marxist, Leo Marx published his *The Machine in the Garden*, with its transformation of Henry Nash Smith's observations about industrial imagery into a putatively out-and-out attack by Melville on capitalism. In a few years—after the political and cultural upheavals between 1965 and 1970—critics began taking it as an undisputed fact that Melville was an author concerned about "the fate of the poor" and bent on "exposing the essence of capitalist society." At the very least Melville, if not yet at a conscious level, was moving toward the "outright condemnation" of "the capitalist mode of economy" that would (supposedly) characterize his later works.[26]

By the 1980s the previously marginal Marxist view had become the common coin of criticism. The action of *Moby-Dick* was now seen as grounded in "capitalist expansion and possession," or in "industrial capitalism." Ahab is obsessed with the white whale because "capitalist appropriation has failed him"; he is "like a disappointed fetishizer of commodities." *Moby-Dick* is once again an "industrial saga" and a demonstration of "class conflict" in which Ahab exploits his "proletarian crew." If anything, Hall's language in 1950, though avowedly Marxist, was more nuanced than this. "The death of the *Pequod*," he had written, "is the ultimate destiny of a culture which holds values that are contradictory to human welfare. If Ahab is a product, in a sense, of the culture and of the machine, he extends the implication to the point of destruction for all."[27] The kind of argumentation represented by Hall's phrase "in a sense" was no longer in evidence in the 1970s and 1980s; instead the unabashed return of the word "proletarian" signaled a revival of the didactic spirit of the 1930s.

If Melville set out primarily to criticize capitalism, as all these critics assumed, it followed that the *Pequod* goes to the bottom of the sea because it is the ship of the American capitalist state. With capitalism in the picture, long-discussed questions about how to interpret the whale's sinking of the

ship dropped from sight. Seemingly forgotten was the observation by earlier critics that even if one narrows the symbolic
meanings of the *Pequod* to its ship-of-state aspect, the sinking
still has ambiguous implications. Was Melville issuing a
prophecy or a warning? What is the meaning of Ishmael's
survival?

In 1964 Alan Heimert had concluded that Ishmael's survival expressed Melville's "undying democratic faith," and
that the American ship *Rachel* that takes him aboard "points
to an American future that is not without charity and not,
perhaps most importantly, without hope." Even Leo Marx
similarly if more darkly wrote that "Ishmael is saved...in
order that he may deliver to us a warning of disasters to
come."[28] But in the 1970s and 1980s the issue was solved
flatly and unequivocally. Ishmael's survival notwithstanding,
the American ship of state deserved (and deserves) to sink,
and so Melville sank it.

The critics had different ideas about exactly which American sins Melville was punishing. For one critic the spectacle
is simply the satisfying one of an "industrial world sailing to
annihilation." Richard Slotkin specifies that the *Pequod* goes
down because of "our devotion to material progress."[29]
Michael Rogin spreads his net wider. "Capitalism, imperialism, and slavery were, at the origins of capitalism, symbioti-
cally intertwined," he believes. The American ship of state
accordingly goes down in retribution for its "greed," as a
result of its fetishization of commodities, because it "en-
grossed half of Mexico," and finally because of slavery and
Indian killing: "those who killed the red man and enslaved
the black met their manifest destiny in Moby-Dick." By
"rooting Ahab's freedom in the enslavement of his crew,"
Rogin further explains, Melville showed that in the American
"so-called free society," freedom was based on slavery. There-

fore even "if the end of *Moby-Dick* imagines the end of slavery, then the price is the destruction of the ship of state."[30]

Robert K. Martin puts it that the catastrophe has to do with slavery conceived as "the blood guilt at the center of American experience." Still, for him as for Rogin, capitalism (a matter of "profits and war") also plays its role. Carolyn Karcher sees Melville as pronouncing a just possibly evadable "apocalyptic judgment that threatens America for her continued enslavement of the Negro." It is more common, though, for critics to regard the coming apocalypse as inevitable.[31]

On the other hand slavery is usually regarded as merely a part of Melville's wider indictment of America. Expressing evident satisfaction, one critic broadly puts it that "the kingdom which raises its Ahabs to command will come to grief smartly." Another has it that Ishmael envisions the coming fate of an "unrepentant republic." (The former critic explains that Melville was showing that the whole idea of America as a "free republic" is a "tragic illusion.") Still another critic, positing that Melville was disillusioned because America had "deserted its principles," concludes that in *Moby-Dick* "the dreaded judgment" eventually "befalls America... because the redeemer nation has become indistinguishable from Babylon."[32]

Other critics believe that *Moby-Dick* is a still wider "critique of Western civilization in its latest destructive incarnation." Here again Leo Marx showed the way. "Throughout *Moby-Dick*," he had written, "Melville uses machine imagery to relate the undisguised killing and butchery of whaling to the concealed violence of 'civilized' Western society." Melville is asking us, one critic of the 1980s concludes, "if we can survive the free [Western] world Ishmael has handed down to us." Putting this view in the most up-to-date terms so far, still another critic explains that "Captain Ahab's monomaniacal pursuit of the White Whale is ultimately motivated by a will to power" characteristic of... "Western logocentric man."[33]

In these interpretations Matthiessen's democratic possibilities have devolved into an unremitting vision of American evil. In the process the possible wreck of the ship of state is reduced from a way of raising questions about an entire nation and its culture to a way of denouncing that nation's (or the West's) production system and its putative excesses. The ship's sinking can only be a punishment for these, the critics of the 1970s and 1980s believe, despite its having been pointed out, among other obvious objections, that such catastrophes are traditional in the epic and tragic writings with which Melville encourages the reader to compare *Moby-Dick*.[34]

In small matters as in large, a uniform rhetoric of stolid denunciation has come to prevail in discussions of *Moby-Dick*. Take the richly allusive doubloon nailed to the mast by Ahab and variously interpreted by him and the members of his crew as they successively step forward to inspect it. In 1970, in recognition that nothing better characterizes Melville's masterpiece than its profusion of multiple significations, an anthology of commentaries was titled *"Moby-Dick" As Doubloon*. But to Leo Marx money simply implied capitalism. Ahab uses the doubloon, Marx had it, because he "concludes" that "his best hope is to exploit the simple quantitative, acquisitive system of value honored by a capitalist society." Once again critics took up the refrain. Ahab's "offering the doubloon as reward for the first sighting" of the white whale was an attempt "to integrate Moby-Dick into... the money system." Or, making the anticapitalist argument in an opposite way, because the doubloon is decidedly *not* "part of the system of capital that commissioned the ship," it deflects attention *away* from capitalism, thereby demonstrating that Melville was not yet as politically radical as he should have been.[35]

With the doubloon, as with other elements of *Moby-Dick*, the critics are likely to offer conflicting interpretations but to refrain from arguing about these inasmuch as they agree fundamentally that, one way or another, some kind of aspersion on America, and particularly on capitalism, is involved. So has it been with the "railroad image" called attention to by Henry Nash Smith. Intones Ahab:

> The path to my fixed purpose is laid over with iron rails, whereon my soul is grooved to run. Over unsounded gorges, through the rifled hearts of mountains, under torrents' beds, unerringly I rush! Naught's an obstacle, naught's an angle to the iron way![36]

Despite the easy assumptions of some critics, Smith showed that these iron rails, like *Moby-Dick*'s other industrial images with "malign" implication, are not employed as part of any antiindustrial or anticapitalist critique. But Leo Marx had nevertheless gone on to pronounce that the iron rails represent "heedless, unbridled, nineteenth-century American capitalism." And so Ahab came to be seen as a hard, industrial or industrial-capitalist "iron" man.[37]

One critic finds that by employing "the language of territorial conquest and expansion," Ahab's speech "illustrates the connection between the capitalist search for wealth and the patriarchal search for power." Another critic similarly has it that we recognize and deplore "Ahab's expansionist voyage." A third critic offers the opposite finding that Ahab "is in the power of the machine." Melville means to convey, this critic believes, "the negative of American hopes that technology would empower free men." The first of these critics well expresses current thinking when he writes that "seeing Ahab's soul as a railroad train may indeed convince us of his determination, but it must also convince us of Ahab's identification with the [malevolent] forces that built the railroad, conquering a continent and subduing nature.[38]

It is evident that virtually any mention of industry, or as in the case of the doubloon, any mention of money will set some people to thinking about capitalism. It does not matter that neither industry nor money is exclusive to capitalism. Forgotten is it that Judas was lured by thirty pieces of silver and that greed, rapacity, and economic exploitation all predate capitalism. Nor does it seem to matter to politicizing interpreters that capitalism is not, to say the least, universally regarded as an evil. Finally, it does not seem to matter that there has as yet been no response to Henry Nash Smith's contention that Melville alluded to capitalism and industry in a haphazard rather than a coherent way.

The same historical amnesia regarding previous criticism prevails in discussions of *Moby-Dick*'s main characters and themes. Starbuck, the First Mate who tries to dissuade Ahab from his mad quest, went from being regarded as "the most admirable" crew member (though some thought they detected weakness in his eventual submission), to being called an "accessory to Ahab's evil purpose." The word "buck" in his name came to suggest "the cash-minded manufactured man." He now exemplified the "sorrowing liberalism" that got America into Vietnam. And his "tragedy is the tragedy of American democracy itself."[39]

In contrast, Queequeg has been elevated from the convenient object of Ishmael's musings on the essential brotherhood of all races and religions, to Starbuck's former "most admirable" status. Although as a harpooner Queequeg has nothing whatever to do with Captain Ahab, one critic believes that "among all the characters only one, Queequeg, is placed by Melville in effective opposition to Ahab." Even though he is a South Sea islander and the son of a king, Queequeg is assumed without question to represent subjugated American blacks and to make *Moby-Dick* a work dedicated to the abolition of slavery. Queequeg anchors book-length interpretations in which *Moby-Dick* is variously made out to be a pacifist tract, a celebration of homosexuality, and if not primarily so at least in part a protest against the treatment of American Indians and the lot of the working class.[40]

One could go on and on with examples of widely accepted politicized readings, each of which has its modicum of truth, yet just as surely acts to flatten out and cut down to narrow political use a work that heretofore shot out richly suggestive sparks of meaning in all directions. "Who aint a slave? Tell me that," asks Ishmael in reflecting on how as a common seaman he was callously ordered, pushed about, and even thumped from behind. "Everybody else," he argues, "is one way or other served in much the same way—either in a physical or metaphysical point of view, that is." His contention prompts one to reflect on all kinds of human coercion. But the critics, convinced as they are that Ishmael has in mind economic exploitation exclusively, stop at the employer-employee relationship. And rather than seeing this relationship as a two-way street, they assume it to be modeled exclusively on master-slave oppression.

Without question Melville had in mind the economic exploitation of American workers, just as with his references to iron rails and the doubloon he meant to evoke first the terrifying power of industrial machines and then the lure of money in a commercial society. This society, moreover, is surely implicated in the looming perils toward which the American ship of state is metaphorically sailing. As for the crime of American slavery, this surely is not absent from *Moby-Dick*. There is even warrant for the claim that at one point a connection is made in the book between homoerotic brotherhood and democracy.[41] Yet taken all together Melville's radical critiques of American capitalism and American democracy convey only a small part of his imaginative construct.

As it happens, privately Melville was by no means the critic of the status quo that his critics assume. He was not, as it has come to be accepted, politically radicalized while writing *Moby-Dick*. Just as he distrusted radical abolitionism and supported the Compromise of 1850, so too did he disapprove of the European revolutions of 1848 that are supposed to have honed his allegiance to the working class. Once one recognizes "Melville's conservative response to the French revolution" of 1848, writes Larry J. Reynolds, one realizes that in *Moby-Dick* he "provides a damning appraisal of the workingman, at least as he exists on the *Pequod*." Indeed, it emerges that Melville has "imbedded the allegory of a group of workingmen incited to violence and revolt by a political radical [Ahab] who plays upon their fear and greed and inspires them to destroy themselves."[42]

Reynolds demonstrates a "tension" in Melville between concern for the humble and attraction to the exceptional among human beings. "Throughout his works," Reynolds concludes, "his democracy expresses itself explicitly in a humanitarian concern for Polynesian natives, Negro slaves, Irish immigrants, common sailors, and the poor and outcast in general, while his elitism implicitly informs the attributes, attitudes, and actions of his main characters, who are socially and intellectually superior to the mass of ordinary men." Reynolds observes that "recognition of this tension in Melville's thought is not prevalent among his major biographers and critics, and, over the years, only a handful of commentators have pointed it out."[43]

It is no wonder that American criticism should be biased toward the egalitarian side of an author who, like Melville, contains opposing impulses. Such a bias flowed naturally from F. O. Matthiessen's emphasis on the possibilities of democracy in the American classics. But in favoring the democratic Ishmael over the authoritarian Ahab, which was certainly Melville's intention, American critics have tended to neglect the attraction in Ahab's sinister, Napoleonic majesty.[44] Post-1960s critics have gone a step further, remaining entirely caught up in Ishmael's passing concerns with particular issues: economic exploitation, slavery, imperialism, and warfare. They ignore that these problems are only the ideational reflections of another kind of questioning in *Moby-Dick*.

Running far deeper than Melville's own moderate politics, this questioning has to do with more than politics. For Melville's ultimate challenge was to things as they are: to social and personal relations, to the Christian worldview, to the patriarchal gods and the place in the universe to which they assign mankind, to the relationship between the sexes. Not the inequities of any particular regime or national culture were Melville's urgent concern but the fundamental inequities of being. He was, after all, writing an epic.

An epic is a work that at once celebrates a culture and explores its deepest contradictions. In *Beowulf* the land and the court of the Danish chieftan, Hrothgar, rest secure from danger thanks to the bravery of his nobles. But every night a monster snatches and kills one of the heroes from the court. Something is wrong, after all. In *Moby-Dick* the nation represented by the *Pequod* rests secure thanks to its intrepidity and resourcefulness. Its heroes subdue nature's most fearsome monster in the farthest reaches of the Pacific. But one of the monsters thwarts them all, killing many and leaving one of their best, Ahab, maimed in body and spirit. Something is wrong here, too. The epic writer suggests that this something is that which lies beyond the aims that his culture has been satisfied to pursue. And he hints at the costs of ignoring or denying this something.

Needless to say, all of the guilts that radical critics would heap upon America can come to mind when the question of the culture's limitations is raised, as it is by *Moby-Dick*. But Melville's ultimate cause of discontent with his civilization is no simple addition of all its crimes, however distressing these may be. Instead the discontent has to do with the ultimate inadequacy of the culture's celebrated achievements. In the America of *Moby-Dick* these are represented by the subduing and transforming of raw nature in the form of the whale to yield light for the lamps of civilized life.

The existential inadequacy of each culture's achievements is symbolized in epic not only by the monster but also by the ultimate fate of the hero who pursues it. As Christopher Clausen observes,

> Gilgamesh will conquer the monster but fail to capture the secret of eternal life. Hector will lose his final battle. Troy will fall. Achilles will die young. Beowulf will overcome Grendel, but when he grows old the dragon will defeat him and doom his people to extinction.[45]

In *Moby-Dick* the catastrophe at the end is not something having to do with the unequal arrangement of cabins aboard the *Pequod*. It is not, that is to say, about class any more than it is about capitalism. Insofar as the *Pequod* represents the American ship of state, class and capitalism are of course part of the picture. But the central meanings lie elsewhere. As Jeremy Ingalls has written, the epic "begins and ends with a selection of events deployed as emblems for the maximum dilemmas of the human soul."[46] The ending of *Moby-Dick* is deployed to suggest that democratic/commercial civilization has not resolved the dilemmas of human existence as well as it thinks. Despite this culture's successes, despite its ability to bring light, it remains metaphysically inadequate before the irreducible savagery of apparently subdued nature.[47]

In any culture the dilemma posed by epic constitutes a challenge. To face the challenge by admitting that some higher purpose may continue to elude the culture can be to take a step in the evolution of a higher consciousness. To ignore the challenge, or to conceptualize it in a narrow manner, may be to forgo the opportunity of taking such a step forward. As the *Iliad* challenged the ancients, and the Bible Christian cultures, so later works, not all of them epics strictly speaking, have challenged particular national cultures. Shakespeare provided the English and *Don Quixote* the Spanish similar opportunities for centuries-long examinations of the national spirit.

The English were in effect presented by German scholars with the works of Shakespeare as objects of the highest kind of contemplation. Similarly the Americans, who ignored Melville for three-quarters of a century, were presented by the Englishman D. H. Lawrence with *Moby-Dick* as a worthy object of their attention. Both the English and the Americans redeemed their neglect by making their own the works that had been presented to them in a new light. For some forty years after D. H. Lawrence's revelation, American criticism of *Moby-Dick* was conducted as an act of cultural self-criticism and hence took its place alongside the most serious critical dialogues of other cultures. After the 1960s the higher criticism of *Moby-Dick* withered, having been replaced by political sniping.

In the process *Moby-Dick* did indeed become an intolerable allegory. Where readers and critics had sensed a criticism of the culture for its having missed some ineffable part of human existence, critics came to regard the problem posed by *Moby-Dick* as something palpable and external. Nothing could have been more inappropriate to the epic ambition of Herman Melville. His vast work in effect fell into the hands of Lilliputians, to be cut down to their own size. As for American literary culture, serious discussion about its single uncontested masterwork was interrupted. This meant that whatever contribution the literary community can make to the evolving national consciousness was severely interfered with. Surely no other literary development could have been more unfortunate for American culture.

THREE

Billy Budd: Criticism as Assault on Authority

IN THE 1980s the academic interpretation of Herman Melville's *Billy Budd*, a short novel that had inspired a certain amount of debate over the years, shifted almost entirely to the view that the story actually means the opposite of what it says. No scholarly discovery nor any new critical insight justified this remarkable turnabout. Instead the dubious side in a debate triumphed by default as defenders of a commonsensical understanding all but disappeared from the scene. The reasons for this outcome had less to do with literary analysis than with culture and politics. For at issue among the critics was not so much Melville's story as its implications about the power of the state.

In *Billy Budd* an ingenuous young sailor aboard a British man-of-war must be hanged when he strikes and kills an officer who has brought false witness against him. The contrary-to-commonsense reading holds that Billy Budd did not have to die. He was inadvisedly hurried to his death by the ship's captain, Edward Vere, whose psychological pathology is said to be the real if not ostensible focus of the author's interest. Though the story makes it clear that Vere justifiably condemns Billy to death, critics, starting in the 1980s, routinely argued that Vere's application of the law is arbitrary and unnecessary, that it springs from twisted psychological motives, and that it reflects the inherent cruelty of his privileged class.

In contrast to the critics' emphasis on Billy's sentence, the story itself concentrates on the concatenation of circumstances surrounding that sentence. John Claggart, the master-at-arms who falsely accuses Billy of conspiring to mutiny, happens to be a rare example of the human capacity for pure malice. He is outraged at some impenetrable depth by Billy's equally rare ingenuous spirit. At the same time he is perhaps perversely attracted to Billy's beauty—and made all the more resentful for being so.

Billy's very innocence tells against him in the peculiarly loaded circumstances of the tragedy. For his shock at Claggart's accusation renders him incapable of refuting it. As for the third main actor, Captain Vere, his very insight into the likelihood that Claggart is lying contributes to the disaster. Reasonably enough, he acts to expose Claggart by ordering that he repeat his charge directly to Billy. What Vere cannot know, however, is that Billy has a stutter, that it will overcome him under the shock of the unexpected accusation, that in his frustration he will convulsively strike out at his false accuser, and that the blow will prove fatal when Claggart topples over and strikes his head on the deck.

Appalled, Captain Vere exclaims: "Struck by an angel of God. And yet the angel must hang." His words express the realization that Billy's killing blow stemmed from a rare, radical innocence, but that this kind of innocence cannot preserve him from punishment. In the first place Billy's deed, like Claggart's accusation, forces Vere to treat the threat of mutiny seriously. The most extensive mutinies in British naval history have just been put down. England is at war with France. There is no telling how a ship full of impressed men—Billy is one of these—will react in an engagement with the enemy: something that may take place at any moment. And so, perilously separated from the fleet as he is, Captain Vere decides that, lest any hint of vulnerability be conveyed to the men, Billy Budd, whose fate is sealed in any case, be hanged forthwith. The following morning Billy is duly hanged from the yardarm, having first loyally pronounced the words, "God bless Captain Vere!" The captain, gripped by the tragic circumstances, never forgets the incident and dies in battle with Billy Budd's name on his lips.

Melville penciled a comment on the last page of *Billy Budd* under the words "The End." Not every word can be clearly made out, but Melville's view is nevertheless evident. He considered his story "not unwarranted by what sometimes happens in this incongruous [?] world of ours," namely that one finds "innocence and infamy [infirmity?], spiritual depravity and fair repute."[1] Whatever the exact words, it is clear that Melville has in mind the contrast between Billy and Claggart—"innocence" vs. "spiritual depravity." The best guess is that Melville is commenting on how these radical opposites can go undetected in the world. But whatever he is saying about how oddly the world can work, he hints at no ambiguity in his presentation of character in the story. The story's depths are achieved by the atmosphere of biblical allegory and tragic fate in which its unequivocal characters move. Billy as innocence is bound for an almost Christ-like martyrdom. Claggart as Satanic evil will undermine Billy, whose aspect suggests Adam as well as Christ. Vere as a dutiful Abraham will be forced to sacrifice one of his sons.

Turning this scheme on its head, the academic critics make Captain Vere the villain in the tale. Because in their opinion he should not have had Billy hanged, *he*, instead of Claggart, is said to represent the depravity that can destroy innocence. The critics do not deny that Vere is treated sympathetically or that his actions are defended. After all, it is simply incontestable that Melville presents him as a man of admirable balance: brave but modest, firmly in control of his men without being overbearing, studious without being pedantic. But the critics argue that this presentation is actually ironic. They hold that the reader should judge Captain Vere, and judge him severely, by reversing the meaning of everything favorable said of him, and by taking literally everything unfavorable.

Until 1949 no such possibility occurred to either common readers or professional critics. Alike they experienced a tragic tale involving the radical evil of Claggart, the equally radical innocence of Billy, and Billy's philosophically suggestive imperfection—his stutter—bringing on a catastrophe. A thoughtful, sensitive Vere was caught in a tragic conundrum, and a quasi-religious transcendence of human categories was achieved by Billy in the moment of his death by hanging. Needless to say, dramatizers of the tale for the opera, theater, and movies had no inkling of any lurking irony: to have reversed the picture, changing heroes to villains and evident meanings into their opposites, would have left their stagings without dramatic point.

On the other hand *Billy Budd* is an admittedly difficult work to read. The aged Melville employed an intricately qualified phraseology every bit as involuted as the notorious late style employed by Henry James just a few years later.

(Melville finished writing in 1891.) Not surprisingly, critics of the 1950s, taken up as they were with the study of irony and ambiguity, found in *Billy Budd* a rich occasion for speculation. One after another of Melville's qualified statements about and even criticisms of Captain Vere were first called attention to in that decade and proposed as indications of ironic authorial intent.

Something of a *Billy Budd* controversy developed and was prolonged thanks to the circumstances under which the work was written, published, and received. In his last years Melville, having become a virtually forgotten figure, had taken to publishing himself privately. He died in 1891 without preparing *Billy Budd* for the printer. In 1923 his confusingly penciled-over manuscript was published in a somewhat defective transcription that would later complicate criticism. In the meantime, *Billy Budd*'s philosophical tone struck its first readers, for whom the salient fact about Melville was his having been forgotten in old age, as a triumph over neglect. The previously rebellious Melville seemed to have "sailed into a mildness," as W. H. Auden phrased it in his poem "At Melville's Tomb," and to have left a final "testament of acceptance," as an early critic put it.

Later critics would refine this view by noting that Melville came not so much to accept fate supinely as, according to F. O. Matthiessen, to "respect necessity." He projected not a mild but "a harsh and difficult acceptance." Ignoring such nuances, though, other critics kept reacting against the passive implications of the earliest readings. Instead of being termed a "testament of acceptance," they argued, *Billy Budd* ought to be called a "testament of resistance."[2] The new phrase, among other things, contained the opinion that Melville remained the upbraider of destiny he had been in his youth. Since he supposedly carried forward his attitude into

Billy Budd through ironic reversal of the apparent meaning, the antiacceptance interpretation of that work is referred to either as the "resistance" or the "ironic" (sometimes "ironist") reading.

In 1962, in the midst of the controversy between the two readings, previous defective transcriptions of the confused *Billy Budd* manuscript were substantially improved by a scholarly edition. The most striking change was the removal of the story's preface. In this brief paragraph the significance of the "momentous" year in which the story takes place—1797—is laid out. The French Revolution, the paragraph states, had promised "the rectification of the Old World's hereditary wrongs"—wrongs the reader will soon witness in the impressment of Billy Budd and be reminded of when mention is made of the 1797 Nore and Spithead mutinies in the British navy. But then the paragraph goes on to say that "the [French] revolution regency as righter of wrongs itself became a wrongdoer, one more oppressive than the Kings." This authoritative opening statement disposes the reader to place the English, antirevolutionary Vere on the side of right and to regard the existence of such practices as Billy's impressment as actually supporting rather than discrediting Vere's cause, inasmuch as they would eventually be reformed (as were the practices that resulted in the Nore and Spithead mutinies).

The paragraph in question, though, was shown to have been used as a preface in error and was discarded. Captain Vere was not decisively supported at the outset as had been thought. A still later edition, in 1976, restored the questionable paragraph, placing it further on in the story. By this time, though, it should have become evident that the preface was not crucial, after all, since the narration amply sets forth the same justification for England and for Vere. Nevertheless, the impression lingered that the discrediting of the preface in 1962 favored the new resistance-ironic reading.

So too with Melville's revisions. The 1962 editors Harrison Hayford and Merton Sealts had shown that Melville, working in his typical fashion, had incrementally added complexities in successive rewritings of *Billy Budd*, the last one of which added lines in which Vere's subordinate officers voice doubts about his conduct. On the other hand the editors pointed out that Melville also added exonerations of Vere at the same last stage. Nevertheless, a second misleading impression was created—namely, that at the time of his death Melville was moving toward discrediting Vere.

In academic literary disputes there is never an adjudicating body to pronounce on the issues or even to decide what they are. Published contentions about literary works can be noticed, ignored, or credited as each professional reader sees fit. Arguments may be dismissed, accepted, or disputed, again as individual critics see fit. Accordingly, just as the 1962 edition of *Billy Budd* could misleadingly leave impressions favorable to the resistance reading, so resistance essays on Billy Budd could continue to exert influence for years after their arguments were refuted. For these reasons, and because of the editorial issues, it took some twenty years, until 1968, for the major arguments about *Billy Budd* to be thoroughly sifted.

In the meantime, evaluations continued to be written from what might be called the commonsense point of view— namely, that the narration meant what it said. The resistance/ ironist argument, advanced for the most part by academics who had never earned critical stature, seemed destined to fade quietly into obscurity. It was true that the ironists included in their number Melville's scholarly biographer, Lawrence Thompson. But Thompson was not a literary critic, and his eccentric contention that the narrator of *Billy*

Budd should be seen as "stupid" was not shared by other ironist critics, who in any case tended to disagree with one another in yet other respects.[3]

In contrast to the ironists, the commonsense readers included writers of international stature and, later, leading intellectuals and scholar-critics of the great age of literary criticism from 1940 to the mid-1960s. Joseph Conrad, E. M. Forster, W. H. Auden, Albert Camus, Thornton Wilder, Lewis Mumford, Eugenio Montale, Hannah Arendt, and Lionel Trilling understood the story to mean what it said; so did the scholar-critics F. O. Matthiessen, Carl Van Doren, Yvor Winters, John Middleton Murry, Newton Arvin, R. P. Blackmur, Harry Levin, Charles Feidelson, Marius Bewley, Maxwell Geismar, Richard Chase, Leon Howard, R. W. B. Lewis, Milton R. Stern, Wayne Booth, and Roger Shattuck.

In retrospect, some of the commonsense critics can be faulted for overemphasizing certain elements of the story in accordance with another enthusiasm of 1950s criticism—that for myth and symbolism. But they were uniformly careful to keep either their enthusiasms or their politics from governing their conclusions. Not so the ironist critics, who came to dominate academic interpretation in the course of the 1950s and 1960s.[4] They allowed themselves to treat the story as confirming their own political opinions. For them its supposed disapproval of Captain Vere contained a political criticism of his privileged class. When their case was finally scrutinized and found wanting in 1968, they did not bother to respond to the essay that refuted them.[5]

The myriad of ironist arguments—one later essay lists seventeen points supposedly telling against Captain Vere—actually come down to a single issue: the necessity of trying, sentencing, and hanging Billy. If Vere is not inexorably constrained to arrange these steps, he is most certainly blameworthy. If Vere's actions are defensible, on the other hand, any anomalies in his character and behavior are reduced to relative unimportance. Practically speaking, therefore, in responding to the ironist argument one can put aside everything other than Vere's decision to arrange Billy's trial and hanging. This means that the debate over *Billy Budd* centers on the brief, pro forma, drumhead court meeting called by Vere to confirm that Billy must be hanged.

The officers present naturally want to take into account three things: Claggart's provocation, Billy's likely innocence of the mutiny charge, and the absence of any intention to kill. But Vere explains that neither circumstance nor motive can be taken into account in a military court operating under the Articles of War. The officers then ask if the court can find Billy guilty but mitigate the sentence. No, Vere explains, the death penalty is absolute and firm. Innocent though Billy may be of the mutiny charge brought against him by Claggart, deserving of death though Claggart is, mercifully and understandably disposed to pardon Billy as the captain and his officers understandably are, Billy Budd has committed murder without any visible, nameable, extenuating circumstance such as the military law might allow.

The draconian necessity of executing Billy can be denied only if one is willing to set aside the undeviating strictures of the military law. One branch of ironist criticism is willing to set aside the law as outlined by Vere. Its practitioners contend that the eighteenth-century military statutes governing warships must have made Vere aware that he could have judged and acted otherwise. In the absence of any hint in the story itself that Vere may have misapplied the law, such research can simply be dismissed out of hand. Literary criticism concerns itself with what authors wrote, not with how they might have been more accurate. Criticism may, to be sure, usefully comment on discrepancies between a fictional account and the historical record to which it refers. The author may have committed a revealing slip—naming a wrong king or president—or have intended a minor joke or irony by incorporating an error of fact. But these possibilities are nothing like what the critics assume about *Billy Budd*— namely, that the reader is supposed by Melville to possess an arcane knowledge of eighteenth-century British naval law, and from it to conclude that Vere knowingly violated correct procedure.

As chance would have it, Vere's judgments and procedures, along with his account of the law to the drumhead court, turn out to be historically correct. At the time the story takes place, it would have been virtually impossible for Billy to have escaped hanging under *civilian* law. Melville discussed the far more stringent military law in *White-Jacket*, his 1850 account of "The World in a Man-of-War." In peacetime, he pointed out—and in the relatively lenient American navy—no matter what provocation an officer might commit, every sailor's "indignant tongue is treble-knotted by the law that suspends death itself over his head should his passion discharge the slightest blow at the boy-worm [that is, the young officer] that spits at his feet."[6] In *Billy Budd*'s wartime English setting, instant hanging, rather than the hanging at dawn as arranged by Vere, would have been the most likely result of either disobeying or striking an officer, let alone killing one.

It is just conceivable that the punishment for defying or even striking and killing an officer could have been put off, under special circumstances, for enactment when the ship returned to its squadron. This is the alternative that occurs to one of Vere's officers just before the trial. The best-informed ironist attacks on Vere come down to advocating such a delay, even though Melville is at pains to justify the more usual course taken by Vere of acting quickly. But if actual eighteenth-century naval practice is going to be invoked, then the most likely outcome of putting off Billy's trial, sad to relate, would have been a death sentence in the form of his being flogged through the fleet. This horrific punishment, a flaying alive, always resulting in death and which was almost inevitably imposed for striking an officer, was described by Melville in excruciating detail in *White-Jacket*. It had been imposed on some of the Nore mutineers, whose fates are reported in the naval history cited by Melville in *Billy Budd* itself.[7]

Legal questions aside, to argue that *Billy Budd* should be taken ironically is to argue that, as one critic has been honest enough to put it, this story is "unique in the history of fiction."[8] A few late-nineteenth-century stories present what are known as unreliable narrators: that is, narrators whose self-serving way of setting forth the facts is meant to be seen through by the reader. But there is no contemporary story in which what is claimed about *Billy Budd* exists: namely, that the author-narrator expresses himself in a style that on the one hand reflects his own personality and convictions, yet on the other hand perversely and obscurely—so obscurely that no one notices his intention for a quarter of a century—is meant to be read as revealing the opposite of what he says. Such a story would be a literary curiosity. It would also amount to being a one-dimensional tale of innocence oppressed by cruel tyranny: in effect a literarily uninteresting tract warning that people in positions of authority are liable to abuse their power.[9]

Given the overwhelming case against the ironist reading, its persistence among so much as a minority of critics—let alone its present dominance—would be difficult to explain.

But a remark by Milton Stern (perhaps the leading Melville scholar of his time), goes some distance toward explaining the theory's attraction. Writing against the ironist interpretation in 1971, Stern was concerned to dispel the assumption held by many of its proponents that Melville could not possibly be sympathetic to Vere and Vere's privileged class. Stern demonstrated that Melville, rather than remaining an upbraider of destiny throughout his career, had become increasingly conservative over the years. His sympathy with Vere, therefore, was to be expected. Stern's demonstration was all the more convincing inasmuch as he did not share Melville's point of view. Instead he confessed in his introduction to *Billy Budd, Sailor* (1975), "I find myself in sympathy with the ironist readings although I disagree with them."[10] Stern, it can be said, resisted the ironist temptation. But exactly what was the source of the temptation toward which he confessed himself to be drawn?

Lionel Trilling provided an answer to the question in his novel of 1947, *The Middle of the Journey.* In it, though he was writing before the first ironist/resistance reading of *Billy Budd* appeared, Trilling anticipated the attraction of the thesis. His novel's character, Gifford Maxim, is an American Communist who announces his break from the party in the complicated form of an essay on *Billy Budd.* In the essay he offers a critique of "the modern mind...in its radical or liberal intellectual part." Committed as this mind is to utopianism, he explains, it fails to grasp the deeper realities of life and therefore will have an inadequate understanding of *Billy Budd.* To the liberal mind, Maxim writes:

> Billy Budd will be nothing more than an oppressed worker,
> and a very foolish one, an insufficiently activated one,
> nothing more than a "company man," weakly acquiescent

to the boss. And Captain Vere will seem as at best but a conscience-ridden bourgeois, sympathetic to a man of the lower orders but committed to carrying out the behest of the established regime.[11]

The chief difference between this attitude and the academic resistance reading of only a few years later—aside from Maxim's 1930s-style rhetoric—is that the reader described by Maxim does not presume that Melville himself intended his story to be taken as a political protest.

In his own reading of *Billy Budd*, Maxim focuses on the conflict between "Law," as represented by Vere, and "Spirit," as represented by Billy. (Maxim's use of the word *Spirit*, though evidently intended by Trilling in part to convey Maxim's portentous abstractness of thought, would later appear in actual *Billy Budd* criticism.) Billy's Spirit consists, of course, in his profound innocence, associated by Melville with the Adamic state of man before the Fall. But Billy lives after the Fall, in a condition that Maxim, still in his portentous style, describes as one of "Necessity." The result, as Maxim formulates it, is that "Vere must rule the world of Necessity because Claggart—Evil—exists."

The reader of *The Middle of the Journey* is obliged to think through Maxim's oracular pronouncement. Its point would seem to be that the Claggarts of the world may be offset morally by its Billys, but practically the Billys are not able to deal with the Claggarts in any effectual way. Society therefore has to resort to the rule of law. Necessarily crude and imperfect, the law cannot adequately assess a pure nature such as Billy's—or a purely evil one such as Claggart's. Hence the tragic dilemma of *Billy Budd*: the law, though indispensable, may in the rare case destroy a representative of the very "Spirit" it was instituted to protect. The weight of

Maxim's critique is directed at the failure of the liberal mind to recognize that there is no way out of such a tragic dilemma. "The belief of the modern progressive," he writes,

> is that Spirit should find its complete expression at once. Everything that falls short of the immediate expression of Spirit is believed to be an ignominious moral inadequacy. To such minds Captain Vere is culpable because he does not acquit Billy in defiance of all Law. To them, Vere's suffering at being unable to do so is a mere sentimentality. It is even hypocrisy.

By the "expression" of Spirit, Maxim means simply the triumphing of the good. He is arguing that the 1930s progressive mind cannot bear to accept a setback for the good when, as with Billy, it is powerfully associated with the working class. Later, resistance critics never quite called for Billy's acquittal by Vere in defiance of all law. Yet Trilling, through Maxim, clearly anticipated that they would harbor just such a wish.

Through Maxim, Trilling also exposed a defect of the original acceptance theory. He did so by coloring Maxim's acceptance of Billy's sacrifice with a subtly revealed, smug satisfaction. Maxim grasps the necessity for Billy's death a bit too readily and with too little regret. His initial formulation is sound: even though Billy is destroyed by the Law, his Spirit is preserved because order has been preserved. In such a preservation of Spirit, Maxim persuasively argues, lies mankind's hope for progress—a hope ill-served by the liberal mind's incapability of postponing utopia. Yet Maxim reveals that he is not truly dedicated to Spirit. He is just as desirous, one suspects, of putting off the triumph of Spirit as liberals are of rushing it. Consumed with his insights into the idealistic misconceptions of the liberal mind from which he has freed himself, Maxim, though he would deny it, has actually shifted his allegiance to the letter rather than the spirit of the law.

On the one side, then, Trilling showed that the acceptance reading of *Billy Budd* is susceptible to a rigidly reactionary impulse, while on the other side the resistance reading is driven by an opposite, equally rigid demand for imminent change in the human condition. Of the two, the impulse for change is likely, in the nature of things, to be the more urgently evoked in most readers by the story—hence the greater temptation for the resistance reader to mold the story to his own desires. Melville himself comments on our instinctive attraction to the ideal natural man brought to mind by Billy. That which is "pristine and unadulterated," he writes in *Billy Budd*, always seems to derive from man in his natural, prelapsarian state. In contrast, "the man thoroughly civilized" —which is to say, the man like Captain Vere—has to the "moral palate a questionable smack as of a compounded wine."

From the outset, furthermore, Billy is presented as not only attractive in himself but as virtually embodying the democratic ethos. He acts as a peacemaker aboard his first ship, *The Rights of Man*. Here, partly thanks to him, democracy's dream of creating a political state in which natural man is preserved seems to be realized. No wonder that Billy, who suggests so much more than mere order in society, commands greater emotional allegiance from the reader than either the law or its representatives.

On the other hand Melville does not entirely weigh the balance in favor of natural Spirit over Law, as is often assumed. For *Billy Budd* has to do with *military* law. The draconian absolutes that prevent military law from taking into account the extenuating circumstances surrounding Billy's crime, Melville makes clear, would not apply under civilian law. "Before a court less arbitrary and more merciful than a martial one," Vere points out at Billy's trial, the evident fact that Billy intended "neither mutiny nor homicide" (as one of the officers has put it on his behalf), "would largely extenuate." Generalizations about the rigidity of ordinary law—seen as one of its necessary features by Trilling's Maxim, or as one of its reformable cruelties by resistance critics—do not really apply.

Melville constructed a very special situation in which society, in order to preserve itself from a hostile outside force, temporarily invokes a unique kind of law governing a small minority of its citizens. To be sure, some critics, recognizing the uniqueness of the situation, have not hesitated to condemn English society for arming itself with martial law. The same society, they can point out, is also shown to perpetuate cruel injustices like Billy Budd's impressment. In addition, the protest against such injustices in the recent mutinies that Melville makes much of were "fanned by flames from across the sea"—in other words, were inspired by the French Revolution against which Billy and his impressed shipmates are forced to fight. The revolution, Melville has admitted, purposed "the rectification of the Old World's hereditary wrongs," and "to some extent, this was bloodily effected." Why not, then, a resistance reading of *Billy Budd* based on rejection of retrograde England?

It is possible to advocate such a reading so long as one recognizes that Melville himself did not share it. Instead he emphasized that Billy would have had no better chance under the Revolutionary French. As Captain Vere points out at the trial, "the enemy" (France) also has "naval conscripts, some of whom may even share our own abhorrence of the regicidal French Directory." The French conscripts must, like Billy, serve under martial law, which is after all universal. (Martial law was not slated for reform by the French revolutionaries.)

Billy Budd, all this is to say, is not merely about England at the end of the eighteenth century. Nor is it, as some critics would have it, allusively about America in the nineteenth century, though both of these places are included in its reach. *Billy Budd* is about the tragic possibilities inherent in society's invocation of its ultimate power over life and death when faced with an external threat to its existence. If the story concerned an evil society that did not deserve to exist, or a naval officer who acted in a perverse manner, then the whole point would be lost. The society would be bad, or the military officer would be bad, but the conundrums of power in all human societies would not be at issue. As a result, the story would have little resonance.

Oddly enough, those who conclude that society is in fact being condemned by Melville because it kills Billy Budd fail to ask themselves how absolutely they really maintain their objection to such a sentence as the one Billy receives. Trilling in effect raised this question in the chilling conclusion to the chapter on *Billy Budd* in *The Middle of the Journey*. He has a liberal-progressive, fellow-traveling husband and wife typical of well-meaning intellectuals of the 1930s contemplate Maxim's essay. Given their views, both are naturally repelled by its defense of Billy's sentence, but on one point they shockingly support what they take to be one of the essay's purports:

"If you think about it," said Nancy, "you see that it is really quite applicable to the Moscow trials. Even if those men were subjectively innocent—I mean even if they had good motives for what they did, like Budd—I don't believe that that's so, but even if it were so—they may have had to be executed for the sake of what he calls Law in the world of Necessity. And you remember how they all concurred in their punishment and seemed almost to *want* it. Certainly before they died they had a proper appreciation of Law. They realized that the dictatorship of the proletariat represented Law."

When it comes to apologizing for executions by the state, Trilling is pointing out, the same liberal mind that professes an absolute dedication to Spirit has provided the world with examples of willing acquiescence and even unsolicited apologetics for the murder of innocent individual spirits committed for reasons of state.

The resistance reading anticipated by Trilling could not in the nature of things take the specific 1930s form he gave it of treating Billy as a worker and Vere as a boss or exploiter. Instead resistance readings eventually began to take on the coloration of 1960s radicalism. Stimulated by the concept of innocent youth punished by paternal authority, critics in the 1960s imagined Melville to be finding fault with "the system," by which they sometimes meant the law and sometimes the "tragic guilt" of society itself. The demise of Billy, wrote one critic willing to put not too fine a partisan political point on it, was a "triumph of political evil, of conservatism." It followed that the story meant not only radically to champion "the people" but also amounted to "a call to rebellion."[12]

As for Captain Vere, he became either the sixties paternal equivalent of the capitalist exploiter, or an "organization man" (a fifties term still in circulation), or an upholder of the status quo, or simply a rigid authoritarian. Vere seemed no less distasteful in the 1970s, but some resistance critics did begin an attempt to find a way out of having to maintain that *Billy Budd* is to be read ironically. Under the influence of poststructuralism, it began to be suggested that *Billy Budd* was uninterpretable. Either Melville had written an imperfect story, or an ultimately meaningless story, or else he had left evidence balanced so as to be both for and against Vere, in which case the story functioned as a kind of Rorschach test in which the reader "exposes his own nature" in judging it.[13]

For the most part the resistance/ironist reading continued to hold sway in the 1970s. Summarizing critical opinion in 1975, Barbara Johnson could quote critics who called Vere "authoritarian," "stupid," "cowardly," "vicious," "perverted," and "criminal." One can add that by this time Vere was routinely being held personally responsible for Billy Budd's death. He was a "martinet" whose "persecution" of the innocent young sailor was variously explained as a "monomania," as "sadomasochistic," or as "primitively" inspired. Vere's speech to the drumhead court came to be described as "one of the most wicked uses to which rhetoric has ever been put." Vere himself was described as "this war criminal," and was compared to a "commandant of a concentration camp."[14]

Resistance critics were not embarrassed to join in what could with justice be described as a ganging up on Captain Vere. On the contrary, instead of recognizing that they reflect a consensus, most revilers of Vere contrive to present themselves as dissenters from a supposedly dominant sympathy for Vere. In fact such sympathy grew increasingly rare in the 1970s and 1980s. In the meantime, though, within the resistance orthodoxy the proliferating analyses and explanations for Vere's conduct were beginning to contradict one another. In addition, eccentric propositions, such as the one that Vere and Claggart are equally depraved characters, became commonplace. At the same time *defenses* of Claggart also became common.[15] No theory, no matter how farfetched, was challenged so long as it claimed to support the resistance reading.

In the 1980s, revealingly, the generalized opposition to authority of the 1960s and 1970s came to express itself in *Billy Budd* criticism in a more explicitly expressed political radicalism. The terminology of the 1930s used by Lionel Trilling's characters began to appear in actual criticism. *Billy Budd* became a conflict between members of "a ruling class" and "the common people they oppress." One critic explained that "the social group" to which Vere belongs "is largely responsible for what happens." As for the nation-state of which this group is a part, it operates under "a bankrupt moral system." Vere ultimately represents what amounts to a "military state" resting on a "police power" and a "war machine."[16]

The "system" these critics have in mind turns out to be not so much the English as the American one. Melville may have written about eighteenth-century Great Britain, but Vere's ship, the *Bellipotent*, is said to be an "apt" name for America. One critic commits a revealing slip by arguing that, after killing Claggart, Billy should have been removed to another "American" ship. For another critic, Melville's story "fore-shadows...the triumph of militarism and imperialism in America." The guns on Vere's ship should be regarded as having historically "evolved" into the aggressive missiles of what yet another critic terms the American "war machine." Moreover, Captain Vere's mustering of his crew on deck should call to mind "the giant Nazi rallies," and hence, almost needless to say, America.[17]

Once the analogy with America was established, yet more extreme political views proliferated. One critic argued that because the sailors accept Billy's sentence, they are like the [American] citizenry, cowed into uncomprehending, submissive apathy, [which] gives the captains of government and industry a free hand with the deficit, pollution, the arms race, the whole, huge, unholy, terrifying mess."[18] What began as a self-indulgence of *Billy Budd* criticism—allowing one's political sensibilities to influence interpretation of the story—reached a logical conclusion: politics came to dominate interpretation.

Ironically enough, no sooner was the radicalizing of the resistance interpretation accomplished than its practitioners began to find their own rhetoric unsatisfactory. One of these practitioners was Bruce Franklin, a radical critic who condemned "those who misread the story"—that is, read it as written—for having "terrifying values."[19] Franklin did not reveal how he would treat fellow politically radical critics of the past—among them Maxwell Geismar, F. O. Matthiessen, and Newton Arvin—who figured prominently in establishing the acceptance reading of *Billy Budd*.

Nor did Franklin seem to be aware that he was in effect also condemning his contemporary fellow radicals for too vigorously adopting the resistance reading. Yet this is the implication of his somewhat rueful conclusion that if Vere is seen as "an especially tyrannical, unjust, irrational, brutal, or ignorant captain, his act [that is, of condemning Billy] could be ascribed to his personal character rather than to the military and imperialist institution of which he is, by his own argument, merely an officer." In other words, too much denunciation of Vere can prove to be politically counterproductive. In fact, as other politically radical critics have begun to realize, ascribing *any* guilt to Vere interferes with the political use of *Billy Budd* by narrowing the focus from the governmental system to an individual.[20]

Liberal resistance criticism, unlike its radical cousin, does not have as its primary purpose the discrediting of American institutions. Yet any resistance reading, often without realizing it, amounts to a repudiation not just of the particular authority that happens to be responsible for Billy's execution, but of governmental authority in general. As one Marxist critic pointed out: "To read Vere literally is to accept the existing system of authority. To read Vere ironically is to undercut it."[21] Should a resistance reader admit, explicitly or implicitly, that an existing authority can be legitimate, his reading would be fatally undermined. For it is always conceivable that legitimate authority may have to act to preserve itself by wielding the most extreme form of punishment at its command. It then becomes possible for there to arise a circumstance in which a death sentence could prove to be legitimate in principle but repulsive in practice. In such a situation one would have to recognize the crude limitations of authority yet reluctantly concede its ultimate legitimacy. This is precisely what Melville confronts the reader with in *Billy Budd*.

To say that one "accepts" *Billy Budd*, therefore, is hardly to express complacency. On the other hand to "resist" the logic of *Billy Budd*, paradoxically enough, does lead toward complacency. For by assuming that there is a way out of the dilemma posed by Melville, and by denouncing Captain Vere for not taking it, the resistance reader spares himself the philosophical and moral conundrum posed by the story as written. Acceptance therefore proves to allow more scope than so-called resistance for the full play of disturbing emotions stirred up by Melville's carefully wrought dilemma.

Among the painful implications with which the acceptance reader must struggle are the story's negative implications for democracy. To be sure, it isn't democratic America that is designated in the story, despite claims by radical critics, but England. Yet Melville calls England at the time *Billy Budd* takes place "the sole free conservative power in the world." Of course, in the political culture of American universities, where "conservatism" is equated with "political evil," the phrase has been taken to condemn England. Read without prejudice, though, it solicits the reader's allegiance on behalf of England against Revolutionary France on the grounds of England's maintaining a representative, or "free," government. (Here it is that one can properly describe *Billy Budd* as having reference to America, whose government is also a free one.) At the same time as England is endorsed, its hanging of Billy casts doubt on the efficacy of free institutions and hence on the American nation's conception of itself as the perfection of English freedom.

In the Old World, in an absolute monarchy such as that of tsarist Russia, Billy could have been saved—as he could be in a modern totalitarian state. A member of Captain Vere's class in an absolute monarchy would be free to act arbitrarily to pardon or even reward Billy if he saw fit. As for the crew, it would interpret such an arbitrary suspension of the law not as a sign of weakness (as Vere worries it may in the wake of recent mutinies), but as an expression of power—of the very principle of absoluteness on which such a state rests. Only in constitutional states such as Great Britain and the United States does a departure from legal procedure present itself as a breakdown of the system.

As a young nation America has from the outset been represented symbolically by ingenuous young men comparable to Billy Budd. In contrast to the Old World's practice of hemming in its citizens with formal, legal restraints, America theoretically trusts in the unfettering of such individuals. But America has chosen at the same time to apply to them and others the English tradition's respect for the law in a more pure and equitable fashion. With cruel irony, this respect and this purity turn out to be exactly the forces that doom Billy. Melville seems to be suggesting that a kind of iron necessity in human affairs renders permanent the law's built-in insensitivity to the essence of the individual. With the best will in the world, it follows, a democratic state will always harbor the same capacity to violate innocence as any other political system.

Resistance readers, insofar as they have considered this conundrum of democracy, have taken it as a call for reform. Historically this is apt: as Frederick I. Carpenter pointed out in 1953, the American democracy did go on after Melville's time to include the tempering of justice with mercy even in its martial law. But the Melville of *Billy Budd* was no reformer such as he had been early in his career; rather, he had become a conservative pessimist. Ignoring the evidence of Melville's shift to conservatism both in his life and in *Billy Budd*, resistance readers have continued to view him as interested in correcting an inequity. Instead he was pointing out a tragic limitation in human affairs.[22]

To resistance readers it seems that to accept Melville's plot is to adopt the view that the givens of the law cannot and should not be altered. But acceptance implies only that the plot of Billy Budd as Melville devised it cannot be rejected: given the circumstances laid out, Billy must die. (Acceptance by no means requires adopting the view of the early critics who read the story as an allegory of acceptance by Melville of his neglect by the public.) Acceptance of *Billy Budd*'s plot, this is to say, need not imply acquiescence spiritually in its outcome. Indeed, resistance within a framework of acceptance is entirely possible. Such resistance might charge Melville with something akin to the *Schadenfreude* of Trilling's character Maxim, who welcomes the catastrophe of innocence in *Billy Budd*.[23]

So framed, the debate over *Billy Budd* could rise above the crude *ressentiment* to which resistance critics have reduced it. Commonsense critics could defend Melville's assault on the progressive impulse as disinterestedly realistic and not Maxim-like. Resistance critics would respond in their turn, expressing in one way or another their reactions to the story's seeming refutation of the progressive impulse. But so long as resistance critics unnecessarily deny the plain sense of *Billy Budd*, they succeed in illuminating only their own willingness to distort literature in the interests of repudiating authority.

F O U R

Huckleberry Finn: The Return of the Genteel Tradition

UPON ITS PUBLICATION in 1885, Mark Twain's *Adventures of Huckleberry Finn* was banned from public libraries, and Huck Finn's bad language and behavior were subjected to high-minded censure. One hundred years later, in a similarly Victorian manner, Huck's wavering attitude toward race and slavery were deplored, and once again the book disappeared from public libraries. While today no one would deny that Mark Twain's presentation of the slave, Jim, is disturbing and embarrassing, and while the values that later critics of the book wished to instill are superior to the shallow moralism of the 1880s, these later critics, no less than their predecessors, have violated a work's literary integrity by demanding that it conform to a particular morality. Their air of offended virtue in response to racism in *Huckleberry Finn* has returned academics of the 1980s—ordinarily priding themselves on being iconoclastic if not outrageous in their moral attitudes—to the spirit of the genteel tradition.[1]

The genteel sensibility dominating nineteenth-century American literary taste called for socially acceptable attitudes expressed with strict propriety of language. Huck's asocial attitudes and colloquial language, both of which manifestly violated genteel standards, led straight to the Concord Public Library's banning of the book in which he appeared. Yet the genteel tradition was dead by the turn of the century, and both Huck's table manners and Mark Twain's literary manners ceased to seem outrageous. Instead they came to be appreciated as triumphs of literary realism.

Still later *Huckleberry Finn* was elevated to the status of a work deserving advanced literary discussion. In introductions to paperback editions in 1949, T. S. Eliot and Lionel Trilling treated it as both symbolic and mythic. In the course of the 1950s other critics, having been shown how contemporary critical terminology could be applied, proceeded to flesh out the accounts by Eliot and Trilling. Huck Finn's escape from the stifling life of his small Missouri town was viewed as a journey toward an idealized brotherhood with the escaped slave, Jim. The raft on which the two of them floated away was more than a raft, and the river whose current swept them along was more than a river. Trilling spoke of the river's "noble grandeur in contrast with the pettiness of men," and he suggested that the river took on the attributes of a god, which "to men of moral imagination, appears to embody a great moral idea." That idea obviously included a condemnation of slavery—so obviously that the condemnation could go virtually without saying. Eliot put it that by allowing the reader "to make his own moral reflections," *Huckleberry Finn* delivers "a far more convincing indictment of slavery than the sensationalist propaganda of *Uncle Tom's Cabin*."[2]

Also in the 1950s, though, genteelism—minus its concern for propriety of language—returned to American criticism as an approved attitude toward racism, and Mark Twain's novel again fell into disgrace with literary critics. Leo Marx, for example, was not satisfied with the reader's own moral reflections. In 1953 in his essay "Mr. Eliot, Mr. Trilling, and *Huckleberry Finn*," Marx chided both critics for their complacency toward Mark Twain's "glaring lapse of moral imagination" in the book's final adventure, where slavery is treated lightly.[3] For years this adventure has been criticized as tediously long, and both Trilling and Eliot conceded its defects. But they argued that the formal aptness of the book's return to the atmosphere of its opening section rescued matters sufficiently to sustain the claim that on the whole *Huckleberry Finn* deserves to be regarded as a first-rate work of the literary imagination.

The opening section, it will be recalled, features the "boys' adventure book"–like misbehavior of Huck and his friend Tom Sawyer. Huck, the nondescript son of the town drunk, has agreed to live with a respectable widow, go to school, and learn manners in order to get in on Tom's latest game: forming a gang of pretend robbers. Huck's father, though, abducts him and returns him to his slothful, irresponsible existence. When Pap Finn gets so crazily violent with drink that he threatens Huck's life, the boy runs away to nearby Jackson's Island. There he stumbles across Jim, a recently runaway slave well known to Tom and himself. Huck and Jim find a driftwood raft and set off down the Mississippi.

The next to the last of their adventures is the takeover of the raft by the two confidence men who call themselves the Duke and the Dauphin. When these scalawags run out of luck and money, one of them sells Jim back into slavery. Again Huck and Jim run away, but this time they are separated, and Huck ends up at a farm coincidentally owned by Tom's Aunt Sally and Uncle Silas. The gullible couple takes Huck for Tom, whom they have never seen and who is momentarily expected to arrive for a visit. Huck as usual plays along, letting them believe he is Tom. When Tom himself arrives, after being alerted by Huck he pretends to be his own brother, Sid. The boys soon locate Jim, who is being held locked up on this very farm, slated once again for a return to slavery.

Tom now conducts one of his make-believe adventures, an elaborate and unnecessarily involved plot to free Jim, even though a few minutes' work at night could easily do the job. In fact Tom knows, as everyone else at the farm does not, that Jim has recently been set free—something Tom reveals only at the end. It is Huck's participation in Tom's doubly unnecessary rescue shenanigans that has always disturbed critics and has threatened the book's stature as a classic. In the course of his adventures Huck had learned that contrary to the South's slaveholding ideology, Jim is fully a human being. But now Huck's hard-earned appreciation of Jim's humanity is no longer evident.

The aesthetic shortcomings of all the coincidences and late revelations, and the diminution of stature of the characters, troubled Leo Marx less than the neglect of what he considered "the theme at the novel's center." This was the "quest for freedom" from slavery for Jim and all others of his race and condition. According to Marx, this is the theme actually being developed through Huck's gradually dawning appreciation of Jim's humanity. But Mark Twain suffered a "failure of nerve," charges Marx; he let Huck regress to his initial, stereotyped view of Jim (and at the same time returned Jim to his initial, equally stereotyped behavior). As for Eliot and Trilling, they were guilty of taking the theme of freedom from slavery altogether too "lightly" by discussing the shortcomings of the last adventure in aesthetic rather than moral terms.[4]

In order to make his case against *Huckleberry Finn*'s treatment of race, Marx had to challenge Eliot and Trilling's mythic interpretations. He began by labeling Eliot's account of the river "extravagant." The book's critique of slavery should be located not there, he argued, but in an action: Jim's run to freedom with the aid of Huck. Marx himself made clear the function of his shift in emphasis from the realm of the mythic to specific actions. His was an attempt, he wrote, to restore some of the social consciousness of the 1930s-style, leftist criticism against which Eliot and Trilling seemed to him to be overreacting. From a leftist point of view, Huck and Jim can be seen as rebels whose actions criticize and whose spirits reject society as it is.

Somewhat contradictorily, though, Marx offered a second account of the book's theme, this time implying that the social message was not actually located in the actions of the characters. In this account the raft is "the symbolic locus of the novel's central affirmations"—a formulation that in its emphasis on symbol rather than any explicit action could have been made by either Eliot or Trilling. (Marx did not explain why it should be critically correct to assign a broader meaning to the raft but critically "extravagant" to assign broader meanings to the river.) Marx identified the raft's meaning specifically with Huck's often-cited remark that "what you want, above all things, on a raft, is for everybody to be satisfied, and feel right and kind towards the others." Instead of taking this in the usual way as an expression of genial unconcern with principles, Marx treated it as a "human credo" that "obliquely aims a devastating criticism at the existing social order."[5]

The criticism presumed to be implied in Huck's words supposedly had to do with slavery. That is, the idea of people feeling "right and kind" toward one another evokes other people enslaving one another. For Marx, Huck's credo marked a stage in growth toward his decision at the end of the book to light out for the "Territory," supposedly because he can no longer bear the slaveholding society of the American South. On the way to the book's ending, Huck's famous decision to go to hell rather than turn in Jim is taken to be "the climactic moment in the ripening of his self-knowledge"; at the very end Huck is not escaping petty harassments but portentously traveling "west ahead of the inescapable advance of civilization" (and therefore slavery). Yet Marx ultimately expressed disappointment with his own symbolic raft. That conveyance, he wrote, "provides an uncertain and indeed precarious mode of traveling toward freedom," instead of offering an alternative, positive social vision—as he believed a symbol in a book should do.[6]

Following Marx, critics of *Huckleberry Finn* would go on to voice similar disappointments for the next forty years. Gradually at first but unmistakably by the end of the 1960s, Marx's updated, 1930s-style conception of the book as a social document came to dominate criticism. The essential subject was confidently taken to be slavery and freedom. And the only question to be answered was how well Mark Twain stuck to this subject. The mythic and symbolic interpretation of literature exemplified by Eliot and Trilling was everywhere set aside (though it sometimes crept back in, as with Leo Marx's raft). Nor was the shift to the social approach deterred when its assumptions were thrown seriously into question in 1962 by one of the leading scholars of Mark Twain and of American literature.

Henry Nash Smith challenged placing slavery at the very

thematic and symbolic center of *Huckleberry Finn*. Doing so, he wrote, "presupposes first, that the question of slavery as an actual institution in the Old South is central to the entire novel, and second, that Huck has matured in the course of the narrative so that his last decision has a depth not characteristic of his attitudes and actions at the beginning. Huck's maturity, according to this view, now enables him to perceive that slavery is evil."[7] Neither of these suppositions, Smith went on to show, can stand up to critical scrutiny. Jim's escape from slavery constitutes the overt action of *Huckleberry Finn* but not, as Leo Marx had it, "the theme at the novel's center." And Huck does not grow "in stature throughout the journey." For not even in his famous go-to-hell decision, in which he chooses damnation over betrayal of Jim, does Huck show himself "capable of arriving at the abstract proposition, 'Slavery is wrong.'" Instead Smith wrote, "what he is trying to escape from is not a society corrupted by slavery, but the same petty harassments he had fled from at the end of *Tom Sawyer*."[8]

In 1977 Kenneth Lynn called attention to the phenomenon of Henry Nash Smith's critique having been all but universally ignored—and ignored without so much as acknowledgment that there were grounds for disagreement on both the issue of the centrality of slavery and of the depth of Huck's philosophical understanding. Lynn sided with Smith and added his own objections to interpreting Huck's decision to "light out" as a social critique. Lynn then attempted to account for why critics held to Leo Marx's view. Critics of the 1950s, Lynn observed, had wanted among other things "to believe that Huck was renouncing his membership in a society that condoned slavery because they themselves did not wish to live in a segregationist America." An admirable social impulse had distorted critical judgment by placing an inordinate emphasis on slavery.[9]

This is not to say that society goes unscathed in *Huckleberry Finn*. Huck the renegade is most certainly running from its constrictions. But Leo Marx did not include among these the attempts by Aunt Polly and other benefactors to make Huck a proper member of society by getting him to keep regular hours and wash behind his ears (the stuff of the book's comedy at the beginning and again at the end). Instead Marx saw Huck's ordeal to be his exposure to Aunt Polly's and others' hypocrisy about slavery. Marx's *Huckleberry Finn* was a work neither comic nor meliorist but rather so steeped in outrage at slavery that its fussy Aunt Polly deserved to be called "the Enemy." And with "their shabby morality," Tom's sweet, bumbling Uncle Silas and Aunt Sally Phelps were "reminiscent of those solid German citizens we have heard about in our time who tried to maintain a similarly *gemütlich* way of life within virtual earshot of Buchenwald."[10]

Marx's expression of outrage, though it came in 1953, anticipated the tonality of criticism in the sixties. By invoking the historical fact that all Southerners lived within a slave system, it is possible to stigmatize every single character in *Huckleberry Finn*. Accordingly, the overtly vicious characters—Pap Finn, the murderous Grangerfords, and the duplicitous Duke and Dauphin—came to be treated by white critics as hardly distinguishable from the good characters. As for the good characters, any one of them could come under equal critical disapproval. Tom, for example, came to be seen not as foolishly romantic in his charade of freeing the already free Jim, but positively villainous. As with Captain Vere in *Billy Budd*, once critical admiration soured it did not take long for

Tom—the book's "true central character," according to one detractor—to begin to be hated.[11]

Chadwick Hanson typified the prevailing climate of critical disdain for virtually every character in *Huckleberry Finn* when he wrote in 1963: "If the reader has learned anything from this novel he has learned that the consciences even of the decent people have been depraved by their moral blindness to the evil of slavery."[12]

In the 1980s the kindly Judge Thatcher was condemned. Eventually, logically enough, so was Huckleberry Finn himself, on account of his cooperating with Tom to humiliate Jim in their last adventure. Not even Huck's moral high point was excluded from the indictment. "His decision to 'go to hell' to free Jim," wrote one critic, "is the last shudder of a psyche hopelessly divided against itself and poised for a fall into Tom Sawyer"—than which, it goes without saying, nothing more degraded can be imagined.[13] That Mark Twain had failed to sustain the antislavery vision of his novel seemed incontrovertible to post-sixties critics. One of them, John Seelye, published a well-received rewrite of the entire book titled *The True Adventures of Huckleberry Finn*, in which he brought the plot into line with contemporary thinking about race. Among other changes, Aunt Sally's mild husband, Silas Phelps, was transformed into a vicious hunter of escaped slaves.

Leo Marx and antislavery theorists after him were necessarily at some pains to explain why it was that Mark Twain himself had failed to treat his characters and plot the way they themselves would have. Regarding the characters, Leo Marx explained that Mark Twain "understood people like the Phelpses, but nevertheless he was forced to rely upon them to provide his happy ending."[14] In other words, Mark Twain must have agreed with twentieth-century critics that all white

Southerners of the antebellum period were monsters, and only the exigencies of his plot or his failure of nerve kept him from depicting them as such.

But Mark Twain used characters like Uncle Silas and Aunt Sally Phelps for more than a happy ending. Harold Kaplan, writing in 1972, pointed out that the ordinary folk in the book "cannot be finally overturned, because in a sense they are the only possible authorities; they are, in effect, the 'people.'" If everyone is evil, Kaplan was saying, there can never be a way out of social crimes like slavery. This is why, contrary to most critics' wishes, the book depicts what Kenneth Lynn described as "fundamentally decent people." (Thinking back on the effects slavery had on his own parents and neighbors, Mark Twain expressed an opinion in keeping with this characterization. "I think it [slavery] stupefied everyone's humanities as regarded the slave," he wrote, "but stopped there.")[15]

As for the kindly, selfless Uncle Silas, Mark Twain's portrait of him veers, if anything, toward the sentimental. Far from representing universal evil, he is held up as a good-hearted type of the sort that, we are told, could be found throughout the South during slavery days. No wonder that Michael Egan, a Marxist who unreservedly hates the book's ordinary bourgeois characters on principle, had no difficulty in recognizing that they are cast in a favorable light. He concluded with disgust that they are "the real heroes of *Huckleberry Finn.*" Writing from a different point of view, Alfred J. Levy, one of the rare critics who still argues for the essential goodness of the ordinary characters, has written that Mark Twain "refuses the gambit of making all Southerners knaves or fools because they accepted slavery. Had he done so the book would have become strident propaganda."[16]

As with Mark Twain's failure to depict his characters as the critics see them, so with his failure to arrange the plot as they see fit. Here, surprisingly enough, Leo Marx invoked George Santayana's critique of the late nineteenth-century "genteel tradition." In keeping with that tradition's spirit of conventionality, and in fear of hazarding his reputation as a popular humorist, Marx conjectured, Mark Twain had shied away from the radical implications of the indictment his book was making. In contrast, though, James M. Cox argued that Mark Twain had no reason to be fearful of the genteel tradition: "In saying that the ending of the book discloses a failure of nerve and retreat to the genteel tradition, it seems to me that Marx is completely turned around. Surely the genteel Bostonians [among whom Mark Twain lived and wrote] would have applauded the moral sentiment of anti-slavery and political freedom which the novel entertains."[17]

The Civil War was over, Cox was pointing out, so that it hardly required nerve to express antislavery sentiment (especially among genteel Northerners whose sentiments had always been abolitionist). No more did it require nerve, it can be added, for Marx and other twentieth-century critics to rail against slavery. On the contrary, it was very much in the spirit of the genteel tradition for them safely to do so. Their insistence on the unequivocal denunciation of slavery may have the appearance of a politically concerned challenge to genteel acceptance of the status quo. But in its adherence to currently acceptable social attitudes it turns out to be a form of self-congratulation—in other words, a return to the genteel tradition.

Today's antislavery critics, in fact, respond conventionally to the one element of genteelism with which Mark Twain himself can be justly taxed: his adoption of the sentimental formula in nineteenth-century boys' books, wherein the bad boy turns out to have a good heart. Henry Nash Smith showed how this sentimental cliché lurks even in Huck's crucial "I'll go to hell" scene (against which Leo Marx measures and finds wanting the remainder of the book). In it "there is a covert suggestion," wrote Smith, "that Huck is dramatizing himself, that he has an inkling of the falsity of the moral stance of his conscience."[18] That is, despite pretending otherwise, Huck knows that his decision to help Jim is morally right. Proclaiming his willingness to go to hell therefore has in it a touch of self-dramatization just slightly out of keeping with his undeniable purity of motive.

Smith's analysis need not seriously undercut a scene that he himself agrees to be "one of the high points of our literature." But his analysis does expose the chief critical hazard presented by *Huckleberry Finn*: the temptation for the reader to find in the book expressions of his own enlightened attitude toward slavery. Smith calls attention to the way post–Civil War Northerners indulged themselves in "complacency" and "intense self-righteousness" regarding slavery. That Mark Twain shared these attitudes is evident from his enthusiastic participation in gatherings at which politicians flattered postwar audiences by evoking the evils of the slave system they had defeated. For all his ability to shock his contemporaries, Mark Twain was, as Santayana remarked in his essay on the genteel tradition, susceptible in part to its sanctimonious lures.[19]

Susceptible, too, have been those modern critics who express disappointment at Mark Twain's failure to achieve a higher moral purpose. It is as if, infected by the slight element of cant in Huck's go-to-hell speech, they have come down with after-dinner cases of righteous high-mindedness. To be sure, the critics are not wrong about slavery. But they fail to detect how they have come to use it for their own self-aggrandizement. As a result they have lost sight of how slavery, for all its importance in *Huckleberry Finn*, might be subordinated to a larger conception of freedom.

In the years following Leo Marx's essay of 1953, race indisputably grew to be a central issue in American politics and society. As it did, the antisegregationist wish of 1950s criticism evolved into progressive wishes typical of developments in the sixties, seventies, and eighties. First, Lionel Trilling's saintly Jim began to seem too passive. William Van O'Connor, for example, complained as early as 1955 not only that Jim was badly treated in the last adventure but also that he was saddled with a minstrel-show-like gullibility earlier in the book.[20]

In the sixties' atmosphere of emerging black pride, the emphasis shifted. Jim's "innate dignity" began to be insisted on, along with the "dignity and force" of his dialect. Chadwick Hansen argued, for example, that if one understands the conventions of the minstrel show, Jim actually transcends his buffoonish status. For in the minstrel show: "Mr. Bones, although he seems at first to be abysmally ignorant in comparison to Mr. Interlocutor, is actually very clever and usually wins the arguments, just as Jim does."

In the same spirit, Jim's apparently mistaken contentions in arguments with Huck that Solomon was not wise and that a Frenchman is not really a man, were taken actually to express a deeper philosophical and humanistic perspective than Huck's. J. C. Furnas devastatingly put it that these interpretations of Jim's arguments were attempts to "inflate Jim into a figure from an anti-racist WPA mural." In other words, they were propaganda, not properly literary criticism. As for Jim's undeniably demeaning posture in the last adventure, in the sixties this was explained as an act of self-preservation. That is, once Jim is away from the raft and returned to his slave status, he has, as the critic Michael J.

Hoffman put it, no choice but to reassume his "slave traits," just as Huck must resume his acceptance of society's attitudes towards slavery. Both decisions illustrate how "the forces of society are stronger than the individual's will"—another formula in the spirit of the 1930s criticism that Leo Marx wished to revive.[21]

In the late sixties there was yet another reversal. Black activists had begun to find expressions of sympathy on the part of whites patronizing, and this new perspective in turn made its way into criticism. Huck's very befriending of Jim became suspect, and resentment at the demeaning of Jim reasserted itself. Resentment returned, that is to say, among white critics, who have not let go of it since the late sixties. Black critics of *Huckleberry Finn*, however, tended to have a different attitude. In 1984 the *Mark Twain Journal* asked nine black critics to contribute to a special issue, "Black Writers on *Adventures of Huckleberry Finn* One Hundred Years Later." In their essays none of the critics expressed any doubt that Jim was demeaned, nor was there any question that this circumstance disturbingly reflected racism on Mark Twain's part. But despite their pain at the humiliations Jim undergoes, these critics did not doubt, either, that the reader is given "the author's most powerful evidence of Jim's humanity." Earlier, Ralph Ellison had observed: "Twain, though guilty of the sentimentality common to humorists, does not idealize the slave. Jim is drawn in all his ignorance and superstition, with his good traits and his bad. He, like all men, is ambiguous, limited in circumstance but not in possibility....Jim...is not simply a slave, he is a symbol of humanity." One of the critics in the special issue similarly asserted that Jim is elevated in stature and in fact is set apart "from everyone else in the novel except Huck." As a result,

Jim emerges as "a man, like all men, at the mercy of other men's arbitrary cruelties."[22]

For white critics, in contrast, Mark Twain's treatment of Jim had grown so unacceptable that it began to raise the question of whether *Huckleberry Finn* could be regarded as a first-rate work of literary art. Leo Marx had not quite dealt with this question, though his repudiation of everything that happens once Huck and Jim float past Cairo, Illinois, amounted to rejecting virtually half the book. Critics who rejected still more than this—notably (despite Chadwick Hansen's defense of it) the minstrel-show-like treatment of Jim in the early chapters—were in effect rating *Huckleberry Finn* very low indeed in the scale of literary value, little as that might have been their intention.

The way out of having to devalue *Huckleberry Finn* was provided by a theory that also emerged in the late 1960s. It proposed that rather than suffering a failure of nerve, Mark Twain, especially in the ending, intended an ironic, antislavery, antiracist allegory of the post–Civil War Reconstruction period. He wrote *Huckleberry Finn* during this period, it was pointed out, even if he set its action before the Civil War. Moreover, as he wrote, the freed slaves were being duped and humiliated in ways that could be compared to Jim's treatment in the final adventure (when Tom keeps from him the news that Miss Watson has set him free). The "Reconstruction reading" permitted critics to treat the negative stereotyping of Jim as part of a charade: an ironic imitation of a period of history. The purpose of Jim's treatment was now said to be the exposure of Reconstruction as a sham and deception perpetrated on the freed slave.

But the credibility of the Reconstruction reading depended on its being a correct interpretation of both history and a literary work. Since the reading assumed an ironic intention, furthermore, Mark Twain had to have intended it. As it happens, many historical interpretations of Reconstruction emphasize the gains made by the freed slaves. And as for Mark Twain himself, he never gave any inkling, either within *Huckleberry Finn* or in comments on it, that he intended an ironic allegory. If he did intend an allegory, he did not seem to the Reconstruction theorists themselves fully to have grasped its point. For one thing, Mark Twain remained, as the Reconstruction theorist Neil Schmitz put it, "ambivalent" about Jim. That is, he depicted the cruel irony of Jim's fate after being set free, yet he insulted him with a condescension apparently no better than that directed at the former slaves during Reconstruction.[23]

Earlier critics had offered a convincing if unsettling explanation (which continued to be held by black critics) for this condescension: rather than being ironic, Mark Twain was himself racially condescending. If he was capable of creating the first fully human black character in American literature, he was also capable of treating that same character in terms of racist caricature. Indeed, it is known that he took particular delight in his portrait of Jim in the last adventure, selecting the most humiliating passages for stage readings to promote the book. Not even his touring partner, George Washington Cable, probably the most progressive white intellectual of the period on the race question and a fierce denouncer of Reconstruction-style racism, objected.[24]

Reconstruction theorists have for the most part ignored Mark Twain's known attitudes. Some of them do try to account for his apparent innocence of any ironic intention by theorizing that he was in effect seized on by the temper of the age unconsciously to create the ironic allegory they favor. But if this was so, just what the allegory points to, besides Reconstruction in general, becomes an open question. Do

Tom and Huck, as one critic suggests, represent the do-gooders who caused harm under Reconstruction because of their unconsciously patronizing attitude toward the freed slaves? Or do Tom and Huck, as other critics contend, stand for the out-and-out racists who climaxed the Reconstruction period by instituting the South's Jim Crow laws?[25]

Given the problems inherent in the Reconstruction reading, it seems surprising that its advocates could not content themselves with advancing a less assailable but equally moral contention: that it is appropriate to remember Reconstruction when thinking about Mark Twain's novel. Whether or not Mark Twain intended to indict Tom Sawyer for deceiving Jim, the critic has every right to cast Tom's behavior during the last adventure in the dark light of Reconstruction.

Once an allegory of Reconstruction is taken to be Mark Twain's conscious intention, though, the book loses essential elements of its force. Alan Trachtenberg, himself a Reconstruction-reading critic, points out the danger of losing the very idea of freedom that Reconstruction theorists wish to champion. While witnessing Jim's flight down the river, he argues, "as readers we are freed of normal historical ambiguities [such as the mixed record of Reconstruction] in order to accept as a powerful given the possibility of freedom for Jim."[26] The Reconstruction reading takes away this given by making the freedom Jim aims toward nothing but another form of slavery. It thereby forecloses precisely the ideal of freedom it wishes to champion.

The Reconstruction reading, more than attempting to elucidate a text, sought a politically correct position on the slavery issue. It followed Leo Marx's complaint that Mark Twain "might have contrived an action which left Jim's fate as much in doubt as Huck's. Such an ending would have allowed us to assume that the principals were defeated but alive, and the quest [for freedom] unsuccessful but not abandoned."[27] In other words, Mark Twain should have made a social contribution by leaving the reader in a proper political frame of mind: literature should be instrumental; it should do good.

The demand for what might be called "anti-slavery instrumentalism" eventually became the leading motif of *Huckleberry Finn* criticism. Typical was the requirement implied by the critic who asked: "Does the relationship Huck develops with Jim ever have the potential power to counteract the slaveholding psychology?" Not only Jim's relationship with Huck but also Jim's character and fate were now judged according to the degree to which they projected solutions, or at least encouraged enlightened attitudes. The outcome for criticism was inevitable: first, a reduction of literature to use; second, the devaluing of *Huckleberry Finn*. As one critic frankly concluded, "If we demand of our novels that they dramatize the movement toward the resolution of significant human problems, then *Huckleberry Finn* is a failure."[28]

Oddly enough, given the presumed sophistication of professional criticism, the demand that literature aid in the resolution of human problems represents one of the most primitive of literary reactions: the wish that the story turn out differently. Like the unsophisticated spectator at a play who leaps up and warns the characters of impending danger, starting with Leo Marx the critics of *Huckleberry Finn* have acted on a wish that the outcome be otherwise than it is. "Where is the murder in Jim's heart?" asked one critic disappointed by that character's accommodating manner. In the same spirit John Seelye replaced the entire last adventure in his *True Adventures of Huckleberry Finn*. Seelye supplied a scene in which Tom's now vicious, slave-hunting Uncle Silas attempts to capture Jim, who drowns. Here was a proper demonstration of the evils of slavery. Yet presumably this ending would still not satisfy the later critic who expressed a preference for Jim to have been lynched.[29]

Instrumentalism made for open season on *Huckleberry Finn*. In the eighties critics either frankly wished the book different from what it was, or else they found new allegorical meanings in it that corresponded neatly with their own political predilections. Their theories, predictably enough, focused on what they regarded as the chief failings of American society. Roy Harvey Pearce declared that Mark Twain had attacked not only slavery but another kind of exploitation as well. When Huck announces his intention to "light out for the Territory," Pearce decided, the reader is meant to take into account conditions west of the Mississippi as they were at the time Mark Twain was writing. Pearce called attention to the so-called Boomers. These were illegal settlers who were pushing the Indians out of their tribal lands. When Huck says that he is "lighting out" we are presumably meant to think of the Boomers and to take it that Huck actually "means ahead of all those people whose civilizing mission [which is to be deplored] Boomerism actualized in fact."[30]

One critic dealt with the Gilded Age (a period overlapping Reconstruction) as a time of rampant capitalism. He was convinced that capitalism brought "the classic market society form of alienation." True, Huck is not a proletarian. But "as a black slave Jim brings into intense focus the contradiction between humane views of the whole self and the market society view that part of the self can be alienated and as a commodity can be sold for what it will command as labor."

Nor far along down the line of causation in such logic came "the violation of family ties." That "sickening disease" is the real subject of the book. Satirized are "the middle-class family as an instrument of socialization" and an economic system threatening to leave people "with no possibility of human community." Or is it that Huck, as the author of the essay "The Education of a Young Capitalist" has it, is running away from the temptation to become an exploitative, Gilded Age–style "robber capitalist"? There is no way of telling, since the critics have left off disputing one another's interpretations, no matter how seemingly divergent they may be. Critical disagreement need no longer arise inasmuch as critics are in fundamental agreement that, in one way or another, *Huckleberry Finn* indicts American society.[31]

Remarkably, not even consensus on this point has satisfied the most politically concerned critics. For them, slavery and the shortcomings of American society cannot be sufficiently emphasized. Slavery in particular appears to them to have been neglected in critical discussion. Leo Marx himself has been taken to task in this regard: despite his accusations that Mark Twain neglected antislavery and the theme of freedom, Marx should have attacked the entire book. From one critic's point of view, Eliot and Trilling's all but forgotten mythic approach infected Marx and others to the point of rendering even them insensitive on slavery and freedom. Moreover, there is in general too much character analysis of Huck going on, to the exclusion of "an entire social, political, and economic construct" (i.e., a properly leftist, politicized criticism).[32]

Providing the desired political "construct" in question has triumphed not only over old-style character analysis and myth-symbol interpretations but also over history itself. After all, however one may feel about the Reconstruction period, when Jim is set free it is difficult not to recall that the American slaves were also set free. Yet several critics, without being contradicted, have denied that Jim is free. They insist that from a correct historical point of view, the American slaves were never truly set free. In the context of Reconstruction properly interpreted, therefore, as Neil Schmitz put it as early as 1971, "the notion of Jim's 'freedom'" seems actually "obscene."[33]

In James M. Cox's 1966 formulation, modern critics tended to congratulate themselves for opposing slavery by conveniently forgetting that the reader "begins the book after the fact of the Civil War," that is, after the slaves have been freed. In the 1980s critics maintained an equivalent genteel self-approval not by forgetting but by actively denying the same historical fact. So influential was the 1980s denial that James Cox himself proved susceptible to it. Adopting the practice of placing the word *freedom* in quotation marks, he wrote in 1985 that "the travesty of Jim's 'freedom' in the closing narrative moment reveals in a way that no other ending could that he is not free and will not be." Reversing himself on the freeing of the slaves and adopting the Reconstruction reading for good measure, Cox now declared that "deep down we know and know socially every day that neither we nor Jim is free despite the fictions of history and the Thirteenth Amendment."

Displaying the fervor of a convert, Cox went as far in his denunciation of America as any of the younger critics who had come to dominate criticism in the eighties. He declared himself concerned with exposing "the big national lie of freedom." The situation he saw—the year was 1985—was one in which "we are at the threshold of George Orwell's *1984*." The reason? Covert imperialism was stifling freedom. "All this [military] defense," wrote Cox, "is being stockpiled to keep our national freedom secure from the *slavery* of rival political ideologies." He continued: "Mark Twain recognized that the holy American nation, having fought out the battle of good and evil along the lines and under the terms of freedom against slavery, was itself moving toward the goal of imperial power."[34]

Just what Mark Twain knew and just what the United States has become in the twentieth century are legitimate questions. But James M. Cox was not really asking them. He was displaying his conversion to the slavery-centered, anti-American reading of *Huckleberry Finn*.

Roy Harvey Pearce similarly discovered late in his career that *Huckleberry Finn* had a moral function. For him the book's purpose was to provide a perspective for "judging" our lives today—negatively. It is our duty, Pearce was certain, also in 1985, to "know what we have become and measure the [horrendous] cost and worth."[35] Pearce's contribution was to find not only American society wanting when so measured, but himself and fellow readers wanting as well. American racism was virtually ineradicable, and the best a reader of *Huckleberry Finn* could do was to admit his own complicity in this circumstance.

The critic Forrest Robinson went yet a step further, indicting himself and all other readers for what he termed "bad faith." Robinson blamed himself partly for enjoying *Huckleberry Finn* (he should have been more concerned about the treatment of Jim) and partly for suffering over it (in the form of an inauthentic experience of shock at the way Jim is treated at the end). His shock represented bad faith, he explained, inasmuch as it rested on a blameworthy lapse of cynicism toward the racist society depicted. Given what America was and is, he should not have been surprised at Jim's treatment. No less than himself he found Mark Twain guilty, along with Huck, not only of similar cynicism, but also of active racism.[36]

In contrast, black critics once again saw the situation differently. In the essays for the special issue of the *Mark*

Twain Journal, they expressed no doubt about the outcome of the Civil War for the slaves. David L. Smith observed that at the time *Huckleberry Finn* was published, "more than twenty years of national strife, including Civil War and Reconstruction, had established Huck's conclusion regarding slavery as a dominant national consensus. Not even reactionary Southerners advocated a reinstitution of slavery." He might have added that only white academic critics expressed such doubts, and only white critics expressed a need to declare America a failure. For black critics *Huckleberry Finn* remained a work that "reaffirms the values of our democratic faith."[37]

In retrospect, it is possible to see that once *Huckleberry Finn* criticism had been aimed in a moral and political direction by Leo Marx's emphasis on antislavery, the forces were set in motion that would result in Cox's conversion thirty years later. Marx condemned "the tawdry nature of the culture of the great valley" of the Mississippi and its inhabitants. In the sixties and seventies his indictment was widened to what one critic described as "the trivially vicious world of Tom Sawyer's America." At the same time the Reconstruction reading fueled the language of denunciation until Tom Sawyer's pre–Civil War America was routinely treated as continuous with post–Civil War America, both South and North. To discuss *Huckleberry Finn* correctly in the 1980s, as Russell Reising summed up contemporary criticism, required "accepting the continuation of racism and political violence after the Civil War into the present."[38]

The 1950s tendency to let politics color interpretation had developed into a positive admonition to make literature serve politics. Critics are properly influenced, it was said in the 1980s, by "the larger culture's changed attitudes toward blacks." Critics so influenced ought to "freely acknowledge that our reinterpretation is deeply influenced by the dynamics of our culture.[39] No one asked whether critics should be influenced by retrograde changes in cultural attitudes, should these take place. Nor was it noticed that when the progressive dynamic had shifted from favoring irresponsibility in the 1950s to social involvement in the 1960s, Huck went from being lauded to being condemned for his inconsistent, cavalier attitude toward social justice. An essentially continuous attitude of goodwill on the racial question produced changing literary interpretations, often by the same critics, not on account of new interpretive insights but because of a shifting political agenda. The worth of such criticism has amounted to little more than a record of how academic political attitudes have changed over time.

The full intellectual costs of the triumph of genteel, liberal instrumentalizing can only be guessed at. To assess them one would have to take into account the confusions and dubious historical assumptions perpetrated by the Reconstruction reading. To these would have to be added the paradoxical imposition of a wish for *Huckleberry Finn* to encourage reform, combined with such extreme vilification of its characters as to leave not one of them capable of embodying that wish. Yet the most damaging outcome of instrumentalism has been a coarsening of discourse. To set side by side virtually any discussion of *Huckleberry Finn* from the 1950s with most of the criticism written after the late 1960s is to witness a distinct loss of sophistication about how literature works.[40]

In the first place, rendering the problem of the ending a moral rather than an aesthetic question has meant forgetting Van Wyck Brooks's treatment of Mark Twain's cultural limitations. Brooks had argued in *The Ordeal of Mark Twain* (1920) that these limitations resulted in a disappointing inability either to conceive an overall design or sustain a theme all the way through a book. (Brooks thought the cause lay specifically in the provincial conditions under which Mark Twain was born and raised.) When Eliot and Trilling explored the aesthetic failures of *Huckleberry Finn*, they did so not out of insensitivity to slavery but as a continuation of Brooks's cultural analysis.

Once the treatment of slavery was made central, though, discussion of *Huckleberry Finn* was reduced to either moral praise (for its supposedly ironic use of Reconstruction) or condemnation (for its being racist). For those finding racism, morality would seem to require that they dismiss the book as a major work of art. But in practice neither the racist nor the ironic interpretations prove to satisfy their own theorists. Those who attack *Huckleberry Finn* for racism cannot bring themselves to dismiss it as an artistic failure. Those who call it an ironic attack on racism cannot dispel the unmistakable impression that Jim is demeaned by the author himself in the last adventure.

Before criticism grew instrumental it had begun to explore the central philosophical and cultural problem posed by the ending of *Huckleberry Finn*: that the book's American-style rejection of conventional morality does not adequately serve its protagonist in all of the moral problems he faces. The runaway ethos of Huck, for example, contains nothing within it to prevent Tom and Huck's own callous treatment of Jim in the last adventure. James L. Johnson put it this way in his book *Mark Twain and the Limits of Power* (1982):

> The most horrible thing about Tom and Huck is that in the midst of their betrayal of Jim they do maintain a grotesque innocence. There is in them no malice, no desire to harm Jim or to make fools of those around them. They

are simply unconscious of any moral implications that might be attached to their play. Thus, while we may object on moral grounds to the game, our objections mean nothing.[41]

This is, if anything, a more troubling indictment than Leo Marx's. In Johnson's reading, Huck has not forgotten his commitment to freedom, as Leo Marx charged. Instead that freedom, because it is divorced from principle and devoted to the self alone, cannot sustain a commitment to Jim. The question left hanging is that of whence morality can be reliably derived. It is a question appropriate for both litera- ture and criticism. In contrast, the demand for an unequivo- cal antislavery commitment from either Mark Twain or Huck Finn amounts to a relatively crude, and as we have seen, unsuccessful enlistment of literature in a cause.

But is the moral problem of the unfettered self, as it is revealed in Huck's last adventure, actually what Mark Twain was driving at? Johnson tries to answer this by asking why the plot contrives that Huck, though he goes along with Tom's cruelties, "does not himself initiate those cruelties." Johnson suggests that Huck's equivocal position amounts to a strategy: "Mark Twain seeks to avoid an outright condem- nation of Huck, while still pursuing a truth he was reluctant to admit: that to remain a child in the real world was not to maintain a spontaneous benevolence, but to treat others as tools and fools, as playthings to be manipulated and sacri- ficed on the altar of Self."[42] "A truth he was reluctant to admit"—with this formulation Johnson is saying that the last part of *Huckleberry Finn* supplies an action that yields a valuable meaning, and that the author created it; yet it cannot be said that the author fully and explicitly intended the meaning.

Whether or not this formulation proves to stand as a final answer to the conundrums of the book, Johnson has supplied an account that is at once literarily sophisticated and morally sound. The same cannot be said for the stolid emphasis on slavery and race maintained by most critics since the 1960s. Their critical orthodoxy may testify to a generous social impulse. But the spirit of genteel self-approval with which they have imposed that orthodoxy has rendered *Huckleberry Finn* a humorless, charmless work: one lacking both literary force and the moral power to persuade.

FIVE

The Bostonians: Refuting Human Nature

IN 1886 the first readers of *The Bostonians* were disappointed. Anticipating a love story with a due degree of romantic sentiment, they were given instead a controlled satire on feminism and reform. As a result they experienced what James would later describe as "probably rather a remarkable feat of objectivity" on his part, not as a satiric tour de force but simply as a lack of warmth and intimacy.[1] The heroine, Verena Tarrant, for example, is physically attractive and gifted with the spunky liveliness James often captured in his portraits of American girls. But where these other heroines usually shine next to less pure, jaded, and cynical European women, in America Verena's naiveté, ingenuousness, and fresh energy do not quite stand out so as to bestow a romantic aura.

Nor does any special aura hover about Verena's suitor, Basil Ransom. An impoverished Mississippian Civil War veteran who comes to try his fortune in the frigid emotional climates of Boston and New York, he nominally represents the passionate South. Yet in his pursuit of Verena he never quite becomes a romantic lover. Serving as the novel's point of view on the feminist movement, for which Verena becomes a spokesman, he resists the emotional involvement experienced by most of those who attend her speeches. When Ransom woos Verena, the advances and retreats of their sexual fencing are ironically accompanied by their debates about the woman question. This makes the sensible but unromantic point that normal human feelings like those of romance can be distorted in periods when politics becomes a cultural battleground.

If politics has invaded private life in Verena's relationship with Ransom, the personal is projected into the political and social worlds through her relationship with her mentor and intimate friend, the well-to-do feminist Olive Chancellor. This young woman represents the New England reform tradition in its late phase of dealing in ambiguous social issues. Olive is driven by an intense, often conflicted dissatisfaction not only with political arrangements but also with everything from social class to manners to interior decor to men, in whose presence she feels both physically uneasy and morally disapproving. "To her vision," James writes, "almost everything that was usual was iniquitous."

Olive conceives the hope that her own passionate but socially awkward feminist convictions can gain a hearing through Verena's gift for public speech. But as Olive grows attached to Verena, her feminist passion becomes personal. In Ransom's courting, the personal is invaded by the political; in Olive's, the political is compromised by the personal. Ironically, the result is that Olive is more romantic with Verena than Ransom is. Yet the relationship between the two young women can never be satisfactory for the romantically inclined reader inasmuch as Olive's is an impossible love for a member of her own sex.

Whether *The Bostonians* was neglected more because it was satiric or because the object of its satire was political reform, both of these features attracted the modernist sensibilities of the three critics who were responsible for its revival years later. Philip Rahv in 1945, Lionel Trilling in 1953, and Irving Howe in 1956 agreed, as did those who immediately followed them, that James's satire had to do with something significantly amiss in post–Civil War American society.[2]

Howe called this something an American cultural "malaise." In the marginal feminist movement James had found an extreme but representative manifestation of this malaise, centering on "the problematic status of women in modern society." This he "embodied in the often deformed and grotesque sexual lives of the characters, and particularly the women," though the "neurotic and morbid contaminations" of feminism were to be understood as characteristic of all progressive social movements. Rahv, viewing Olive in the perspective of a once-vigorous New England reform movement, saw her as representative of "the sick conscience, of shallow notions and perverse impulses."[3]

Trilling put it that the movement's "doctrinaire demand for the equality of the sexes" sounded like mere colorful eccentricity but became more troubling when it took such distorted forms as Olive's attempt to win Verena in a struggle with the more likely male suitor, Ransom. For James, Trilling concluded, Olive's attempt "was the sign of a general diversion of the culture from the course of nature."[4] Eventually Verena, the young girl who is caught up in a cause and begins to find a vocation in it, realizes that her deeper desire is for a private life with a man she loves. Her political commitment dissipates, and the insubstantial charm of her intimate relationship with another woman is dispelled. In the end, in other words, the natural reasserts itself as mutual attraction reaches across the ideological divide between the lovers and they set off to marry.

This understanding of *The Bostonians* began to come under attack in the 1970s, coincidentally with a reawakening of feminism. In 1978 Judith Fetterly summed up the opposition in her book *The Resisting Reader: A Feminist Approach to American Literature*. In her account, earlier criticism consisted of male critics hysterically attacking Olive Chancellor largely for her lesbianism. "To associate Olive with lesbianism," she wrote, "is, in the critics' eye, to define her as odious, perverse, abnormal, unnatural—in a word, evil." Early critics, Fetterly and others now agreed, had judged Olive too harshly and Ransom too leniently.[5]

To be sure, Olive is the extreme case among the reformers. But James does not satirize her as he does minor characters like Verena's charlatan father with his fake mesmerism, or the vulgarly intrusive newspaper reporter and sycophant of the feminists, Matthias Pardon. Nor did the early critics fail to take Olive seriously. Fetterly had it that F. O. Matthiessen, in treating Olive as "tragic" (in 1947), is "the sole exception to the universal critical attack on Olive." Yet Oscar Cargill praised James's "superb artistry" in rendering her as a "tragic" figure. Writing in 1961 Cargill observed that "the general reaction to her is what it would be in life." That is, she both repelled and evoked sympathy from Cargill and other critics. She suffers from a "pathological selfishness," wrote one critic typically enough in 1968, but eventually "discovers a depth of understanding and courage that is admirable."[6]

On the other hand it is true that one critic, writing in 1966, stated that Olive's "hatred of men in general (and in particular, too, much as she fights against personal dislikes) strikes even the most casual reader as pathological." And another early critic did write that "the novel traces the temporary fulfillment of Olive's hopes and their ultimate destruction when Verena returns to the normal relationship of love for Basil Ransom." Still another critic called Olive "a rather terrifying resultant of Puritanism," and went on to credit James with "artistic and moral courage" for pitting Ransom against the reformers. But despite the expressions of fear and invocations of the natural in some of these remarks, it is hard to regard them as examples of Fetterly's "embattled phallic principle making a desperate stand" inasmuch as all of them were written by women.[7]

The fact is that the gender and time lines that Fetterly wishes to draw concerning attitudes toward Olive do not exist. Unfavorable assessments of Olive, for example, can be found among contemporary feminist critics themselves, including Fetterly. She calls Olive "morbid," says she "has the psychology of the loser," that "Olive believes ultimately neither in herself nor in women nor in their cause or movement," and that she is "her own enemy." Another feminist critic treats Olive as Verena's oppressor, and a third, calling her a "political dogmatist," argues that Olive's attachment to feminism "arises from her own need to get a public sanctioning of her hatred of the male." Still another writes that "lacking humor and charm, obsessive and frightened, Olive is herself frightening."[8]

Ignoring that responses to Olive have always been mixed, and that critics were capable of valuing the Olive-Verena relationship and finding the Ransom-Verena one less than ideal, Fetterly seized on Lionel Trilling's description of *The Bostonians* as a book so full of distorted sexual relationships as to be "suffused with primitive fear." Surveying the writings of so-called phallic critics, Fetterly concluded that "Lionel

Trilling's description of the atmosphere of the novel can be applied with equal, if not greater, accuracy to the criticism of it, for that criticism is indeed 'suffused with a primitive fear.'" The critics had simply agreed that Verena's attraction to Ransom is presented as more natural than Olive's unrequited love for her. But for Fetterly, "the 'argument from nature,' despite all pretensions to the contrary, is simply the biggest phallic gun of them all, used to support an interpretation which is not so much what James wrote as what the critic wants."[9]

Fetterly's political and psychological explanation of phallic criticism—a phenomenon that did not exist—reflects the force with which the very issue of the relationship between the sexes raised by James leaped into American culture and criticism in the 1970s. "If the book is in fact a triumph of the forces of 'nature,'" Fetterly could by then write, the question remains whether "James does not view these forces as odious and in themselves perverse." Earlier critics who assumed James's sympathy with the natural, Fetterly indicated, mistook his true attitude. They offered "no evidence from within the novel" of such sympathy. Evidence about nature, Fetterly went on to observe, was "assumed to be unnecessary" or else was offered in a fragmentary manner.[10] True enough. But the reason is not that evidence was unavailable. It is simply that until the 1970s offering evidence on such a matter would have amounted to a ludicrous belaboring of the obvious.

In the 1970s the obvious became problematic. Some agreed with Fetterly that James himself regarded Verena's evidently natural or biological attraction to Ransom instead of to Olive as "odious." Others thought that James approved, while still others thought that nature had nothing to do with the matter. But if there was disagreement on exactly where James stood, there was none on where he ought to have stood.

Those who put James on the side of nature disapproved of him for it. Those who thought nature had nothing to do with Verena's choice nevertheless thought it a bad one, so that they too aligned themselves against nature.[11]

Despite her complaint about lack of internal evidence, Fetterly attempted to establish James's approval of Olive's planned relationship with Verena exclusively with external evidence (from James's notebooks and letters). When it came to interpreting *The Bostonians* itself, furthermore, she disavowed evidence altogether. To support her interpretation, she explained, she was relying on "a different subjectivity."[12] As far as one can make out her logic, it is that, having proven to her own satisfaction that earlier criticism was ruled by subjective male fears, she is somehow licensed to indulge her own subjectivity. Being of a feminist stripe, this new subjectivity is presumably to be applauded.

A similar approach to earlier criticism led other critics to still further extremes of self-indulgence in discussions of Olive Chancellor's antagonist, Basil Ransom. As with Olive, the older critics had identified in him a mixture of favorable and unfavorable traits typical of James's characterizations in *The Bostonians*. They noted the ironic parallels whereby Ransom politicized his relationship with Verena just as Olive did, was as selfish and possessive as she, and could be as contradictory of his own philosophy when consistency was inconvenient for him.[13] Because the same critics nevertheless accepted Ransom and Verena's marriage, though, they came to be regarded as retrograde in the 1970s. For Ransom had gone from being regarded as the flawed protagonist and not-quite-hero of *The Bostonians* to its unquestioned villain.

The mildest accusations were that Ransom is "selfish" (something formerly said of Olive), "pigheaded," "crude," "rigid," "a liar," "a narcissist," "manipulative," one who acts in "bad faith," shows "infuriating arrogance" and "offensive flippancy," and is a "fool." Taking their cue from Olive's disgusted remark to Verena that men's brutality was given them to overbear even when they see that right is on the feminist side, the critics went a further step to make brutality Ransom's defining characteristic. He was said to display "male brutality," or "right-stuff brutality," or a "brutal hunger for success." He treats Verena with a brutish, "dogged cruelty" and the "sadism" of a "hypocrite and tyrant" or "enslaver."[14]

Escalating still further, the critics saw Ransom as exerting a "satanic effect," and—in taking Verena away to marriage—as committing either a "literal abduction," a "virtual rape," "a murder of some sort," or an "assassinat[ion]." In "berserker fury" he "contaminates" her community of women and destroys "everything in Verena that charmed him."[15]

These reactions resemble not so much literary assessments of a fictional character as personal resentment. For critics who might continue to find attractive Ransom's nobility in military defeat and ponderous but insightful banter, or for those who found him partially flawed, or even pompous and silly, his new detractors' ferocity served as a deterrent—especially to male critics—from treating him in a nuanced way. For example, the aged Charles R. Anderson had the misfortune to be one of the few among earlier critics to have been distinctly favorable to Ransom. After being attacked by Fetterly and another feminist critic for committing phallic criticism by favoring Ransom's "conservative arguments," Anderson, as a third feminist critic put it, "retracted."[16]

In fact he ruefully admitted to having written favorably about Ransom but cannily gave only the appearance of a retraction. Writing in 1985 as though under the eye of a censor, he offered a list of Ransom's virtues with a disclaimer. Ransom has "civility, good manners, charm, tradition and male superiority," wrote Anderson, "all except the last making him an attractive if slightly old-fashioned figure." He then added: "But the last is overriding, a perceptive critic declares," and went on to quote a feminist indictment. Anderson implied but never stated his agreement with this indictment.[17]

Another male critic, though he had not failed to be critical of Ransom when first writing about him, was guilty of an unflattering description of feminism. Alfred Habegger had found that "James offers a harsher critique of the movement" than most critics realized. James saw in feminism "the deadliest sort of selflessness—a selflessness that suspects all personal enjoyment." With historical insight "James accurately catches the impulse in nineteenth-century feminism," Habegger wrote, "that led it to make common cause with the moralistic and repressive temperance movement." Habegger concluded that in *The Bostonians* "the self, denied its legitimate satisfactions and believing itself to be purged of selfishness, develops a monstrous need for power and personal domination. Olive Chancellor enslaves Verena instead of liberating her, and what is worse, convinces her that slavery *is* liberation." Altogether, the Olive Chancellor who for other critics was a compelling, sympathetically drawn, tragic figure was for Habegger a "horrifying" character, "poisonous and suicidal," mouthing "pure cant, sincere yet deceptive, a cover-up of an unconscious malignancy."[18]

As one might imagine, when the cultural winds shifted Habegger was obliged to purge himself far more radically than Anderson. Seeing fit not to mention his earlier apostasy, Habegger indicated little more about Olive than that she was "an extraordinary study in pathology." But "the trouble is,"

he now found, "she is clearly meant to say something negative about feminism and about women." Reborn as a self-
styled "feminist revisionist," Habegger saw *The Bostonians* as
a work of "essential anti-feminism" and "authoritarianism"
deployed with "a sinister design on us."[19]

Habegger now undertook to "resist" (as in the title of
Fetterly's book) the critique of feminism that he had earlier endorsed. Henry James became a "sneering," "haughty author"
whose book suffered from "wretchedly tangled," "clumsy"
sentences and was "in many respects absolutely out of control." Employing Fetterly's "different subjectivity" but calling
it "historicizing" in conformity with the usage of other
feminists, Habegger defended his imposition of an affirma-
tive feminist message on *The Bostonians* by proposing that
James tried to resist the antifeminist implications of his own
book. In the end, according to Habegger's scenario, *The
Bostonians* "had a [nonfeminist] life of its own" that James
could not overcome.[20]

Habegger's conversion was chiefly one of political attitude.
Without substantially altering his assessment of either Olive
or Ransom, he was able to put himself in good odor by
stating that "the trouble" with James's characterizations lay
in their antifeminist intentions. Habegger was exceptionally
frank about putting politics before literature in this way. And
in one form or another his political test prevailed after 1970.
A critic was now judged not by how he interpreted James's
characters or action but rather by how correctly he felt about
them.

Critics could with equal acceptability treat Olive as heroine
or as pathological lesbian. So long as they approved the
former estate and bemoaned the latter, they were in no
danger of being regarded as "phallic." They could judge
Ransom to be treated favorably or unfavorably by James so

long as they applauded or regretted appropriately. They could treat the plot as showing triumph or defeat for Olive, success or failure for the feminist movement, a grim or promising future for Verena—any of these so long as they reacted appropriately.

Those critics who judged *The Bostonians* to be in the wrong about any of the three characters or their fates, or about the feminist movement, usually felt it incumbent on themselves to account for James's retrograde performance. It seemed to them variously a product of his "conservatism," his "masculinist instinct," some psychological aberration, or lack of artistry.[21] If they favored a psychological explanation they assumed that James suffered some kind of psychic disability while writing this particular book—"a nervous, rather hysterical attack on American culture." (Paradoxically, the complaints about inconsistency of characterization came down to disapproving James's treating women characters— Olive and the aged reformer, Miss Birdseye—with increasing sympathy as the tale progresses.) If they favored a lack-of-artistry explanation they called the characterizations inconsistent, the structure faulty, the unreliable narration marked by "prolixity" or "undisciplined expression."[22]

In a hypermodernist variation on these charges, James—or "the narrator"—is assumed to have been as much influenced by his tale as it was influenced by him. In the words of five contemporary critics, James "worries," then "draws back" from the politically radical implications of his tale. He "timidly equivocates," then ends by "refusing to give Olive [here regarded by the critic as though she were a real person] any total epiphany." James uneasily senses that Olive is coming across more favorably than he intended, but he is "impotent" to control his materials. "No more able than his characters" to make sense of his subject, he "becomes oppressed" by radical implications he cannot face.[23]

So much for James's "rather remarkable feat of objectivity." The American writer heretofore regarded as "The Master" by fellow writers and critics is now judged as entirely mastered by his subject. His demotion, furthermore, comes at the hands of academic critics with neither experience nor standing when it comes to the aesthetic evaluation of literature.

The same critics' lack of sophistication in such matters is still more evident in their discussions of Verena Tarrant's character and fate. Should she have married, the critics now ask, and is her marriage going to be happy or unhappy? In an age in which literary criticism is said to have grown almost too abstruse and theoretical to be comprehended, such fan-magazine-level questions somehow enter serious criticism for the first time (albeit from an antiromance rather than romance point of view). The critics absorb themselves in the drama of the Ransom-Verena courtship, lamenting its forward progress in the face of what they regard as overwhelming reasons why it should not succeed. Then, when the marriage comes, with few exceptions they resentfully predict that the young couple will live unhappily ever after.

In the satiric spirit of *The Bostonians*, it is true, James plays up numerous ironies in Verena's attraction to Ransom, especially where it rests on shakier grounds than her relationship with Olive. Literalistically seizing on these ironies, the critics make Verena's story out to be one of "a woman's decline through love." "Defeated" by her love for Ransom, she "embraces a terrible fate." That "Verena falls for nature's ploy" appears as an outrage.[24]

One critic well expresses current incredulity over Verena's choice when he complains that "the narrator can *only* explain her new allegiance to Ransom by revealing that . . . 'It was always passion, in fact [that defined Verena's character]; but now the object was other [italics added].'" How can Verena have shifted her affections to Ransom in this way, he and others wonder? After all, her relationship with Ransom is "more vicious" than her "healthy" relationship with Olive. Ransom simply "wrenches her away from her obligations to Olive, her family, and her audience."[25]

Some critics admit that Olive may have her faults but insist that she is "willing to share Verena with the public," is "constantly aware of her jealousy and her responsibility in her relationship with Verena," and "tries valiantly, against all her own desires, to recognize the integrity of Verena's separate existence." In contrast, "Ransom does not once question his 'right' to squelch the talent, ambition, pleasure and feelings of this person he 'loves.'" Another critic writes, "While Olive is as obsessive and as manipulative as Basil in her relationship with Verena, James shows us that Verena blooms when she is in Olive's company: She is happy and, even better, feels herself to be wonderfully productive under Olive's tutelage." It no longer occurs to critics that even if "all the advantages are with Olive," Verena's choice is part of the human comedy rather than an assault like their own against the nature of things.[26]

At most, contemporary critics modify their disapproval of Verena's marriage by calling it a shift from "one oppressor to another" and of "one kind of captivity for another" (though the Ransom relationship is "more vicious" than the one with Olive). The disapproval of Olive implied in the exchange-of-oppressions formula at first glance appears odd coming from feminist and feminist-influenced critics. But more important for them than supporting Olive as feminist and lesbian, it develops, is combating the impression that *The Bostonians* contains a triumph of nature or implies that a private life in marriage is more "normal"—one critic puts the word in ironic quotation marks—than a life of political agitation.[27]

One contemporary critic does concede, as a "sad fact," that "men and women are incomplete without each other." But she quickly adds that "all unions" are "doomed to be compromises of dominion and submission." Because Verena and Ransom have but an "erotic attraction," according to another critic, and are otherwise "ill suited," they are certain to have an unhappy marriage. James is "seriously concerned" with "the general threat marriage poses to human potential," states the first critic. His novels move toward revealing the "perversity of family and marital relations," and *The Bostonians* is a critique of "the power relationships and unequal gender roles assigned within marriage," state two other critics. If nature does triumph in this book, then, the result is "simply another predictable fall of *woman* to the seduction in the garden, to the slavery of the human race, to 'nature's decoy to secure mothers for the race.'"[28]

Such a remark does not misrepresent the role of nature in *The Bostonians*. Ransom and Verena's union is forged outdoors in nature, during a Cape Cod summer vacation. The plot has pointedly taken the lovers from wintry Boston interiors, to a spring outing in New York's Central Park, to the out of doors on the Cape at the height of summer. Nor are feminist critics mistaken about the ironies that emerge from viewing the courtship as a process in nature. Basil Ransom's inability to support a wife financially grows increasingly at odds with his desire to rescue, possess, and protect Verena. His antifeminist arguments grow weaker even as Verena's logic and damaging insights into the contradictions of his position grow in sophistication.

But what is the status of these ironies and reservations? The imperfections of Ransom and Verena's relationship culminate in the prediction of their future given in the last line of *The Bostonians*. Ransom has come to the Boston Music Hall where Verena is about to address a packed house. Partly to her own dismay, she cannot resist his demands that she give up her career and immediately come away with him. Throwing her cloak over her, he rushes her out of the building, and the book ends:

> "Ah, now I am glad!" said Verena, when they reached the street. But though she was glad, he presently discovered that, beneath her hood, she was in tears. It is to be feared that with the union, so far from brilliant, into which she was about to enter, these were not the last she was destined to shed.

To a remarkable extent this mixed, typically open Jamesian ending has come to bear the burden of interpretation for everything that precedes it. "The final lines," one feminist critic writes, "completely undermine Ransom's victory."[29]

Yet the same critic ably demonstrates that when the scientific Dr. Mary Prance amusedly observes the lovers as if they were part of an experiment, she accurately finds what James terms "the universal passion" at work in them. In other words, she observes that the victory belongs as much to nature as to Ransom. The reader similarly finds in the natural setting in which the universal passion plays itself out an anticipatory gloss on the book's ending. "There were certain afternoons in August," James writes, "long, beautiful and terrible, when one felt that the summer was rounding its curve, and the rustle of the full-leaved trees in the slanting golden light, in the breeze that ought to be delicious, seemed the voice of the coming autumn, of the warnings and dangers of life." The poet Louise Bogan wrote that this sentence "can be set, for sheer power of evocation, against anything in Emily Dickinson."[30]

Among other things, the sentence suggests that the process in which the lovers are caught up is no splendid alternative to the utopian hopes of the feminists but rather an instance of the "terrible," inevitable process of things. Surely the universal "warnings and dangers of life" are what face Basil and Verena as they set off to marry at the end. The tears Verena is destined to shed do not render heterosexual love and marriage untenable. Instead they serve as a reminder from James that the relationship between the sexes cannot be utopianly reordered so as to yield an ideal state of being. Proverbially again, such ideality is neither in nature nor in the contingencies of human life that are its product.

In *The Bostonians* irony is directed wherever nature is denied or not recognized. Contemporary critics take it that feminism is discredited if Ransom triumphs, endorsed if he does not. But it makes no brief for feminism to insist, as the critics strenuously do, that Ransom lacks worldly means or skills or powers, or even outstanding virility. Nor does it matter that his antifeminist theories are undermined by his own shortcomings. The less imposing he is as man and lover, the more clearly nature's design emerges. The young man and woman come together because young man and woman is primarily what they are. Olive and Verena's friendship is "probably as complete as any (between women) that had ever existed" writes James on the one hand, while on the other hand Ransom but exerts "man's larger and grosser insistence." Yet through him nature has its way.

Ransom's brutality consists not in violent behavior but in humanly being a part of nature, as James's own usage makes clear. Sensing his power over Verena, Ransom taunts her with the accusation that she is obliged to tell Olive everything about his wooing. "In playing with the subject this way," James writes, "in enjoying her visible hesitation, he was slightly conscious of a man's brutality—of being pushed by an impulse to test her good nature." Clearly Ransom is not being a brute in the critics' sense of a traducer or torturer of Verena, any more than he is a sexual predator further on when he imagines himself kissing Verena as they sit together on a bench in Central Park—even though one critic regards "this violence" as "a surfacing of male brutality."[31] Instead Ransom is enacting the aggressive male role in a courtship ritual virtually universal in the animal kingdom.

Ransom's being only "slightly conscious" of his biological role in the larger scheme of things undermines his rationalist theories. But the scheme itself is not challenged, except by Olive, whose complaint about Ransom's brutality is satirized, in its turn, as a tilting against nature. An English critic unaffected by current American critical attitudes has summarized the inevitabilities arrayed against Olive: "Verena's relations with Olive are founded on will and can only be kept up by continued application of will; her attraction to Ransom is inspired by all the forces of nature and underwritten by all the romantic conventions." Specifically, James describes Verena's progress as a "fairy tale," and evokes a fairy tale atmosphere as Verena is immured by Olive and rescued by Ransom. Yet feminist critics either ignore the romance theme or, like Judith Fetterly, deny it. "This fairy tale formula," she writes, "of which the critics are so enamored, is Ransom's; it is not James's."[32]

Along with the natural, the normal, and the romantic, critics have come to dismiss the ordinary as it too exerts its influence in *The Bostonians*. The third character in James's triangle, Verena Tarrant, has a fetching appearance and elocutionist-like talent for public speaking that make her an attractive spokesman for the ideas of others. But she is no such extraordinary being as contemporary critics have come to suppose. To call her ordinary, on the other hand, is by no means to denigrate her—as they also suppose. She is simply a lovely, uncomplicated, unneurotic girl. She may not be profound, but she is "quick and ingenious." James calls her "the sweetest flower of character (as one might say) that had ever bloomed on earth." (William James, who objected to his brother's treatment of Miss Birdseye, found Verena "*liebenswürdig*": lovable or amiable.)

Verena is badly served by the now dominant strain in academic criticism with its insistence on the dignity of any and all women. For, once she is conceived of as an important political figure, her choosing an ordinary fate seems to call for an explanation pointing to some extreme circumstance. She must have been violently assassinated by Ransom. If not this, she must be an exceptionally inferior creature: weak of character, "of little value," a "nonentity" whose "vacuous" speeches in support of feminism are the calculated and insincere expressions of a "fool."[33]

Still other critics deal with Verena's decision in favor of marriage by projecting a feminist future for her. Playing yet another variation on Fetterly's "different subjectivity," one feminist critic takes an approach she calls "resistant re- (or is it un-?) writing." Quoting and agreeing with another feminist critic, she concludes that Verena will be unhappy, but her marriage "will educate her to the experience necessary for integrity as a feminist." For still another critic "the novel's ending" implies that Verena "is struggling against Basil as she has struggled against Olive's repressions of the past."[34]

The actual import of the ending is far simpler and more obvious than the ideologically derived extremes imagined by the critics. Ransom's presence at the Music Hall causes

Verena spontaneously to give up "every pretense of a different conviction [from his] and of loyalty to her cause."
"Struggling to free herself" from her mother's embrace, she
shelters under Ransom's protection because, as he correctly
concludes, rather than deliver her speech "she only wanted to
get away, to leave everything behind her." She lets Ransom
hustle her out of the Music Hall. Then comes the significant
line, "Ah, now I am glad!" said Verena, when they reached
the street."[35]

Repeating her word James adds, as we have seen: "But
though she was glad, he [Ransom] presently discovered that,
beneath her hood, she was in tears." These are the tears that
the next sentence, ending the book, pronounces not the last
she is destined to shed. The meaning, surely, is not that
Verena's life is ruined but that it will be less than perfect.
Even as the summer rounding its curve at Cape Cod carried
portents of "the warnings and dangers of life," so do Verena's
mixed emotions at the end suggest that she and Ransom will
live happily and sadly ever after.

Nevertheless, there are critics who deny that an ordinary
marriage is likely to ensue. Others denounce the likelihood
that it will. And virtually all are disgusted by the private life
on which the young couple embarks. That it should all come
down to this ordinary, undistinguished fate seems to be the
main source of current complaint about *The Bostonians*. The
critics would prefer a life in politics for Verena. And in
defense of this preference they have grown willing to alter
the rules of interpretation, to impose their own ideas of how
the book should have been written, and even to dismiss
human nature. No less caught up in their convictions than
James's characters who politicize private life, the critics have
politicized the work in which these characters appear.

The current politicizing spirit could not be more different

from that of the critics who rediscovered *The Bostonians*. For them this was a book that needed to be read with "a full awareness," as Irving Howe put it in 1956, "which means a readiness to admit that it jars many of our fondest opinions." From the point of view of political liberalism James's "cool and ironic misgivings" about reform "may be offensive to our liberal or radical pieties, but there, as James might say, it is." Howe could point out that toward the reformers James betrayed a certain "hard-spirited humor" and a tendency to apply "small measures to large matters, judging difficult social and moral issues by esthetic criteria a little too neat for the job." But rather than being prompted to refute or denigrate James, Howe judged *The Bostonians* to be a "masterpiece."[36]

Howe agreed with the scholars who attributed the initial unpopularity of the book to its wit. As Charles Anderson put it, "American readers in the 1880s lacked the literary sophistication to relish a satire on themselves." Anderson did not reflect—at least not in print—that he had been forced to retract his own relish for James's satire when *his* contemporaries displayed a comparable lack of sophistication. Indeed, they recapitulated what another critic has called the "awful moral earnestness" of a hundred years ago.[37] Once again life became serious. Once again a serious cause undertaken by the enlightened was not to be treated lightly or satirically. Attached to a cause as she is, Verena cannot simply be a bright, attractive girl lucky to escape exploitation (no matter how well meaning). Opposed to that cause as Ransom is, he cannot be an ordinary man whose proposal of marriage and a family represents a normal and therefore acceptable fate (no matter how far removed from progressive do-gooding).

To the morally earnest, Verena's acceptance of Ransom remains a mystery. Despite James's pointedly obvious rendering of her courtship in generic, age-old terms, they cannot help believing that Ransom must have deceived or traduced Verena in some way. Yet the outcome they have witnessed is proverbial at least as far back as Horace's *natura expellas furcâ, tamen usque recurret* ("you may drive out nature with a pitchfork, but she will keep coming back"). The words of a popular song, moreover, express our familiarity with the surprise experienced by those who have been won over: "You made me love you / I didn't want to do it."

Contemporary critics conclude that James must have been a "masculinist" to have endorsed such an outcome. But he was someone who—unlike many of his critics—did not choose such an outcome for himself. He never joined his life with a loved one; he was evidently not heterosexual. That nature's process did not apply to all was something he knew from personal experience. But he was not interested in reducing his art to a reflection of his own peculiar essence. He chose instead to work from the premise succinctly expressed with equal lack of resentment by another nonheterosexual, Cole Porter: "Man must have his mate / On that you can rely."

Contemporary critics strenuously eschew such common-sense understandings. Judith Fetterly, for example, engages Ransom's antifeminist ideas as though they were arguments meant to be taken seriously rather than being in large part expressions of his character. Massing her evidence like a high school debater, Fetterly assails his ideas with heavy irony—as she does not do with Olive's equal and opposite ideas. "With all admirable qualities categorically assigned to the masculine character and hence to men" in his system, she writes exaggeratedly, "and with the feminine equated with the damnable, it is difficult to understand why Ransom wishes to possess himself of any woman, especially one as feminine as

Verena."[38] There is a kind of refutation here, inappropriate as it is to score logical points against a fictional character. But the point is that if Ransom is refuted, it is not so much by logic as by the natural attraction between the sexes. Quite simply, his natural desire to possess himself of a woman is stronger than his theory.

This is not to say that the commonsense, popular-song understanding of how things work exhausts James's meaning. Lionel Trilling had it that *The Bostonians* suggested "the biological nature of moral fact." Marrying and raising a family, when carried out with the purity of dedication James had witnessed in his own mother's life, not only fulfilled a biological imperative but also became a morally beautiful spectacle.[39] In *The Bostonians*, we may say, the biological imperative of attraction between the sexes leads to the morally satisfactory if not quite inspiring marital life to be lived by its young couple. Conversely, the moral aims of the book's feminist reformers do not find an acceptable outcome insofar as they or their sponsors happen to be at odds with biology.

Similarly, Verena's choice of private life over politics—another ordinary commonsense matter—has its moral dimension as well. For politics in a democracy is meant ultimately to serve private life, which is therefore the higher category. And just as humble private life and biological necessity take precedence in the lives of individuals, so does literature answer to something that comes before the causes critics often wish it to serve. This something is the reading experience itself. Just before *The Bostonians* appeared in print James published "The Art of Fiction," in which he rejected the critic Walter Besant's prescription of a moral role for the novel. James did not discuss the critic's role, but his argument suggests that no matter how urgent a literary critic's desire for a better world, his first allegiance must be to the reading experience, and that this experience is in the first place a matter of pleasure.

Paradoxically, the only satisfactory procedure for deriving a moral vision from literature lies in starting with fidelity to pleasure, even though pleasure is not in itself moral. Starting the opposite way—with a moral already in place—violates the ethic of reading and hence, whether or not in the service of a worthy cause, amounts to the commission of a literarily immoral act. With *The Bostonians* the pleasure in witnessing the union of the lovers can, if fully appreciated, be raised to the level of Trilling's "biological nature of moral fact." In contrast, when the reader allows morality to determine his literary response, he places himself in a position analogous to James's pleasure-denying fictional reformers.

Just as the reformers are at odds with biology, moralizing critics are at odds with the primary pleasures of the reading experience. Like Olive with her scorn for all the arrangements of life as iniquitous, such critics have come to disapprove of the ways in which those arrangements are reflected in literature. Where nineteenth-century readers could not enjoy *The Bostonians* because its romance was too cooly presented, the very presence of romance puts off contemporary critics. Of these critics it can be predicted that, because they pit themselves against a fictional representation of universal human experience, they are slated for an Olive-like literary defeat.

It is difficult, though, to hold contemporary critics to account for violating the rules of literary discourse, inasmuch as they explicitly repudiate these rules just as they do nature. Nor can one tax them any more successfully with already published, reasoned refutations of their arguments. They would regard these as part of Judith Fetterly's phallic con-

spiracy to champion nature over feminism. For the divergence between old and new criticism of *The Bostonians* is, as
contemporary critics would be the first to agree, not so much
a matter of interpretation as it is a reflection of an alteration
in fundamental assumptions about life and literature, human
nature, and the nature of discourse. Because *The Bostonians* is
precisely about these fundamental assumptions, the divide
separating its old and new critics stretches wider than with
any other American book. It is difficult to imagine how
critics might once again find common ground on which to
disagree about it.

APPENDIX

Typee: Civilization and Its Malcontents

Typee, HERMAN MELVILLE's slightly fictionalized memoir of his stay among the cannibal islanders of the Marquesas in 1842, was a first, youthful work. Melville went on to write three more books about his seagoing adventures, always improving his skill as a writer. And yet none of these works—not *Omoo* nor *Redburn* nor *White-Jacket*—comes close to recapturing the literary power and philosophical suggestiveness of *Typee*. Not only did *Typee* establish Melville's fame, first in England and then in the United States, but it continued to be read when *Moby-Dick* was forgotten, and still occasions new interpretations, most of them having to do with the question of Melville's allegiance to civilization.

The tale begins when an ill-managed, foul, depressing whaler sails into the bay of a lush tropical island. Two adventurous youths—Melville, who is the book's narrator, and his friend Toby—jump ship and escape into the interior.

Unexpectedly, the highlands to which they flee turn out to be cold and forbidding. They have planned to seek out a peaceful tribe called the Happars and to hide among them until their ship has sailed away. But in clawing their way down from the heights, they stumble into the wrong valley. They find themselves among the Typees: cannibals so fierce they are a terror to all who know of them. Miraculously, for reasons that Melville is never able to divine, he and his friend Toby are given a friendly welcome by this tribe, and they settle down to a life as honored guests. Yet they prove to be prisoners as much as guests, kept under constant surveillance by their hosts and prevented from moving about freely.

Because Melville is suffering from a bloated, apparently infected leg, Toby is eventually allowed to seek help. He is tricked aboard a ship in need of hands, though, and never returns. Ignorant of Toby's fate, Melville cannot be sure of his own. Nevertheless, in the intermissions of his understandable fears he manages to savor the pleasures of what turns out to be a veritably paradisal valley.

There follows the memorable heart of the book. Melville describes a life of lazily sensuous pleasures far removed from his latest contact with civilization: the rigid, regimented economy of shipboard. With a beautiful native girl, Fayaway, he loafs, bathes, eats, cavorts. In paradisal Typee, rules and restrictions come to seem supererogatory. Observing no instances of theft, Melville concludes that he has found an egalitarian society where laws are unnecessary. The only work a Typee performs in the course of his life is the planting of a single breadfruit tree for each of his offspring. This and other fruits are abundant in the lowlands that they inhabit, and the sea yields up its harvest when the men are of a mind to fish. Sensuality is unfettered. The women take several husbands without arousing any apparent signs of jealousy. A physically beautiful people, the Typees live in what looks like perfect natural health. All in all, the chief ills of Western civilization seem to be absent: scarcity, poverty, competition, repression.

The dramatic and philosophical question raised by *Typee* is why, despite all this, Melville decides to escape. When a ship appears in the bay he resolves to show himself. Many of the Typees—the fiercest among them it would seem—now want to prevent him from approaching the water. But for the first time some of them display what appears to be sympathy for his plight and help him hobble and be carried in that direction. They will not let him approach the ship's boat, though, until his part is unexpectedly taken by Marheyo, the somewhat senile old native who has been his host. "He placed his arm upon my shoulder, and emphatically pronounced the only two English words I had taught him: 'Home' and 'Mother.'" This first act of imaginative projection by a Typee is followed by Melville's one act of brutality. He hastily clambers onto the boat. Then, when he is pursued by the horrific, one-eyed chief Mow Mow, who had led the opposition to his release, Melville makes good his escape by plunging a boat hook just below the native's throat.

This richly paradoxical ending creates feelings of both inevitability and regret. Old Marheyo's unexpected projection of sympathy beyond his time-bound world raises the possibility of a genuine meeting of cultures, yet his insight is limited, making Melville's departure seem inevitable. Melville has deplored the Western relationship to the islanders, pointing out how sailors and missionaries brought with them diseases and instruments of war that decimated native cultures. Now his own blow for freedom puts him in just such a relationship to the Typees.

It is not surprising that certain early readers of *Typee* failed to appreciate its ambiguities. Some early reviewers rigidly lined themselves up as advocates for either civilization or primitivism, quite ignoring Melville's balanced distribution of right and wrong, advantages and disadvantages. Starting with the rediscovery of Melville's works in the 1920s, modern critics left partisanship far behind. Then, surprisingly, the terms of the old debate were revived in the 1970s. This time, though, there was no one on the scene to represent civilization.

As a result, *Typee* has come to be regarded by recent critics as an unwavering indictment of civilization, as much so in its ending as anywhere else. Does Melville describe there a scene of agonized parting from Fayaway and her family as he stands on the beach waiting for rescue? This only demonstrates a "betrayal of his loved ones."[1] Is Melville forced into an act of violence to save his life? This "demonstrates the universal trait of savagery." Or, still worse, his act teaches that "civilization has succeeded only in magnifying and developing a basic savagery which is found in a less appalling form in a primitive culture."[2]

Opinions such as these, in which the critics find civilization being exposed as worse than primitive life everywhere in *Typee*, are virtually the only ones currently to be found in academic journals and in books published by university presses. Such publications, it should be noted, are routinely scrutinized and approved by panels of scholars.

Such a loss of confidence in and esteem for civilization is not unprecedented. In *Civilization and Its Discontents* Freud described a built-in resentment at the restraints that accompany civilization. Civilized man constantly chafes against these restraints and is always tempted to repudiate them. During at least two periods in history, Freud suggests, man's accumulated resentments have issued in outright condemnations of civilization. The first of these periods followed the birth of Christianity, and the second the age of exploration. *Typee*, itself a travel book, came at the end of the second period, and capitalized on both contemporary romanticization of the noble savage and a reigniting of the universal urge to flee civilization. It would appear that a third period of the kind drawn attention to by Freud had its birth in the countercultural revolution of the 1960s. One of the fruits of this latter revolution was the repudiation of norms that became a staple of literary discourse in the 1970s and 1980s.

From the beginning those reviewers who emphasized Melville's indictments of civilization spoke in the name of social reform. Writing for the Fourierist *Harbinger* of Brook Farm, the utopian community where Nathaniel Hawthorne had briefly resided a few years earlier, John Sullivan Dwight compared the unfettered, communal existence of the Typees with the evils of civilization arising from economic exploitation. Defending civilization were Christian conservatives stimulated in part by resentment at Melville's criticisms of the missionary enterprise. William Oland Bourne of the *Christian Parlor Magazine* wrote a review that Milton R. Stern, the foremost modern critic of *Typee*, has described as "grim, humorless, and righteous." In it Bourne admits that the bringing of civilization to the islands had its unfortunate consequences. But he accuses Melville of giving a distorted picture by alternately ignoring and temporizing over the "degraded and benighted" practices of the islanders. That such distortion might be part of Melville's literary intention did not occur to Bourne. Nevertheless, he went on to catch Melville in contradictions that can no more be justified from a literary point of view than from a logical or moral one.

The humorlessness and lack of literary sophistication of

Bourne and subsequent Christian reviewers have permitted modern critics to dismiss their arguments. Not so Melville, though, who evidently read Bourne's review with care. For example, Bourne pointed out that in his narration Melville both protested the use of the word *savages* and demonstrated its appropriateness, in one instance following his complaint with an example of native behavior that justified such usage in the very next paragraph. Melville proceeded to remove both paragraphs (along with rephrasings of several descriptions too explicit in their sexual details). These changes appeared in a second American edition a few months after the first. Their fate at the hands of modern editors, a group with no apparent allegiance to either side in the civilization-primitivism controversy, reveals how far scholarly capitulation to civilization's discontents has progressed in recent years.

At Northwestern University an edition of Melville's works based on modern principles of scholarly editing has been coming out since 1968. Its editors have seen fit to reject Melville's revisions. To do so they rest their case, as far as one can make out, on the fact that Melville revised *Typee* at the request of his publisher. Yet the rules of modern editing enjoin acceptance of an author's "final intentions," which is to say his last set of revisions, whether or not they have come at someone else's behest. No rule is without its exceptions, to be sure. But adherence to an author's final intentions is so central to the contemporary editorial enterprise that one is surprised to find an exception being made under almost any circumstances. And still more surprising is it that the breaking of the rule is hardly discussed in the two elaborate and lengthy scholarly essays that accompany the Northwestern edition—essays containing exhaustive discussion and justification for virtually every comma inserted or removed by the editors.

One of the editors candidly reports that in writing to his publisher Melville "strongly implied that his revisions were thoughtful and voluntary." In order to lend "a unity to the book which it wanted before," he had decided to remove those passages that were "altogether foreign to the adventure."[3] In these and similar remarks not cited by the editors, Melville made it clear that he was satisfied with his changes. Subsequently, furthermore, though he had no need to mollify English public opinion, which was put off neither by *Typee*'s sexual explicitness nor its criticisms of American missionaries, Melville attempted to persuade his English publisher to make the same cuts. "The permanent reputation as well as the present popularity of Typee," he argued, "will be greatly promoted by the revision."[4] Yet not even this appeal to the primacy of aesthetic form—something usually dear to the twentieth-century sensibility—could deter the Northwestern editors from rejecting the revisions.

It is a maxim in the study of intellectual history that the faith of each historical period lies hidden in its unargued assumptions. Such is the case at hand. The Northwestern editors assumed that contemporary objections to Melville's remarks about religion or his treatment of sex could only reflect the religious intolerance and sexual prudery of the nineteenth century. Under the circumstances their breach of rules in order to restore passages critical of civilization and religion, along with sexually explicit passages, presented itself as self-evidently enlightened.

In the 1950s Richard Chase, Milton Stern, and a few other critics developed an approach to *Typee* that had the incidental result of honoring Melville's final intentions. For by concentrating on what Melville had termed 'the intrinsick merit of the narrative alone," they effectively made the discursive passages less important. Chase, the author of the seminal *The American Novel and Its Tradition* as well as a book on Melville, was one of the outstanding scholar-critics of his age. Stern is a leading scholarly authority on Melville, and is most recently the editor of a collection of essays on *Typee*. Along with other critics of the 1950s, Chase and Stern began to treat *Typee* as a work of fiction. Scholarship had demonstrated that Melville's account was substantially accurate, its fictionalization amounting for the most part to a heightening of romantic details and a claim to have spent several more weeks in Typee than was probably the case. On the other hand it was possible to argue that Melville the narrator was not quite identical with the Melville who experienced the adventure. The latter, furthermore, introduces himself to the Typees as "Tom," a single syllable that he thinks they will have less trouble pronouncing than his own name. They can only say it as "Tommo," however, and from the point of view of some literary critics the resultant false name given to Melville amounts to his being fictionalized into a character.[5]

Once *Typee* became a fictional work it was but a small step to seeing it as a symbolic one as well. The primitivism-civilization conundrum could now be resolved, not by Melville's philosophizings but chiefly with reference to the needs of Tommo's personal development and through the interpretable meanings of such symbols as his infected leg. So long as *Typee* had been regarded as a straightforward memoir, Melville's leg appeared as simply one more detail of his adventure. Now Richard Chase noted that the leg improved while Tommo enjoyed the pleasures of Typee but swelled up again when the natives threatened to cover him with tattoos. The pain, as Stern agreed, was a call back to civilization.

By treating *Typee* as a fictional and symbolic work, Stern

and Chase were able to remove any unpleasant, chauvinistic overtones from Tommo's choice in favor of civilization. Their approach, however, opened the door to a rejection of this choice by their successors. Thus a typical critic of the 1970s no longer accepted the return to civilization as defensible. *Typee* became nothing more than "a comprehensive satire which unmasks the damned and damning intellect of the Western mind itself." As for Melville's leg, "if the swelling is a symbol at all," another critic writes, "it probably signifies his *attraction* to Typee." For still another critic the pain serves not as a reminder of home but rather "points in fact to Tommo's inability to embrace physicality, an inability which flows from his having been infected by Western consciousness, reason, and intellectuality." And this critic adds: "The fact that Tommo's attraction towards these things is symbolized by a painful infection should be sufficient evidence of Melville's judgment of their ultimate worth."[6]

As these last remarks suggest, once Tommo had been disassociated from Melville, any loyalty to civilization found in the narrative could be dismissed as an expression of his failings as a character. Accordingly, Tommo was now described as suffering from "sexual perversion and self-conceit," and as "selfish and so egocentric that he must impose his will wherever he is." Finally, Tommo is indicted by selective omission in the following account of his escape: "One Typeean does not want to let Tommo leave the island. He swims after Tommo, and Tommo smashes a boat hook into the savage's throat. This, the tale's single scene of violence, concludes Tommo's story."[7] Tommo is the violent one, the swimming native presumably a kind of disappointed host. But in fact the character who "does not want to let Tommo leave" has indicated his reluctance by hurling a javelin at those on board the rowboat Melville has entered. "Swims after Tommo" omits to mention that this native grips a tomahawk in his teeth, leads a group of swimmers shouting their intention to devour the pursued, and is about to grapple the oars—"the maneuver which has proved so fatal to many a boat's crew in these seas."

In retrospect it is apparent that, though by the 1950s one no longer proclaimed the superiority of civilization, one continued to assume it. Thus, consciously or not, when Stern criticized the "primitive savagery of the western ship's crews," he was implicitly measuring their behavior against Western civilized norms, and not those of the South Pacific. Similarly, Stern was free to accept Melville's indictment of the West because he never imagined its being employed to repudiate Western values.

At present the consensus that underlay the original fictional and symbolic readings of *Typee* no longer exists. It has been replaced among literary critics by an unremitting cultural self-loathing. The words *savagery* and *civilization* have come to be used only with quotation marks—"civilization" to separate oneself from a supposedly self-centered, delusory conviction of cultural superiority, and "savagery" to imply that the term is nothing more than an expression of Western ethnocentrism. As one critic explains, Melville "saw that savagery was a term applicable to the Europeans' colonial and missionary activities in the Pacific rather than to the people they practiced upon." At present the only acceptable use of the terms in question is in phrases such as "the savagery of civilization," which is used by another critic of the same persuasion.[8]

It is true that in *Typee* Melville exclaims, "How often is the term 'savages' incorrectly applied!" And Melville also argues that Westerners have "exasperated" the South Sea islanders "into savages." The remark and the argument, however, both appear in the first of the two contradictory paragraphs pointed out by William Oland Bourne. In the remainder of *Typee*, when Melville employed the term *savages*—some two dozen times—he did so in just the manner his own early paragraph complained of. Thus his narration refers to "savage resentment," "the fickle disposition of savages," an ever-present fear of "the savage nature of the beings at whose mercy I was," and "the craft [i.e., craftiness] peculiar to savages." Elsewhere Melville's adjectives are "simple," "unsophisticated," "heathenish," and "treacherous" savages. Given the choice between bringing these references in line with his complaint about misusage and bringing the complaint in line with them, Melville, as we know, chose to remove the paragraphs singled out by Bourne. In addition, he went so far as to strike out the few phrases in his book that were in *accord* with that paragraph: the similarly apologetic "those whom we call savages" and "noble savage" used as an honorific.

As with *savages*, so with *cannibalism*, a seemingly unambiguous term that has acquired both quotation marks and a party of apologists. This time the exaggerated mode of early reviewers was never entirely set aside. Thus with a laudable intent to oppose Western cultural self-congratulation, an anonymous early English reviewer fell into blatant illogic:

> The Polynesians have the advantage of the cannibals of civilised life, for we have long since made the pleasant discovery, that man-eating is not confined to the Anthropophagi of the South Seas. The latter have undoubtedly one redeeming distinction—they can only devour their enemies slain in battle: there is nothing which man in a civilised state has a keener appetite for than his particular friend.

Stern unfortunately perpetuated this kind of verbal imprecision by referring to the scrounging for edibles aboard Melville's ship when stores were low as an example of "western spoilation and cannibalism." This is a highly inaccurate way to describe eating the captain's pig.

Stern's successors, again taking matters further than he could have anticipated, used the same kind of imprecision to emphasize not the inhumanity of individual Westerners but rather the culpability of their nations as a whole. Playing on the same word *devour*, one critic now asked, "Who are the real cannibals, the Typees who practice a ritual of eating the flesh of their dead attackers or the aggressor nations who have come to devour the islands?"[9] But this is not all: cannibalism has also found its positive defenders.

For some critics the self-evident superiority of primitive life is in itself a sufficient justification of the practice. "The Typees occasionally indulge in headhunting and cannibalism," one of them genially concedes. But more important is their possession of the "one valuable commodity of human existence—happiness." More sophisticated critics begin by reducing cannibalism to the status of a literary trope: "the narrative's central metaphor for the primitive's threat to consume Tommo's contemporary identity." One such critic, who has already indicated that he is dubious about the very existence of cannibalism among the Typees, concludes, "Whether or not the Typees are literal cannibals, they are certainly figurative cannibals that are devouring Melville's historical identity."[10]

When it comes to cannibalism the fictional Tommo, who has already been impugned on other grounds, is judged to be so hysterical on the subject that his testimony can be safely laid aside. "There is no evidence the Typeeans actually plan to eat Tommo," one critic states with equanimity. Writes another, "He can never rid himself of his fear of their reported cannibalistic practices, although, in fact, he experiences only comfort at their hands."[11] Five recent critics agree that the true problem lies in Tommo's own character. Critic number one has it that in his estimate of the Typees, "the impulse to fix on the practice of cannibalism as typifying their character is presented as a feature of Tommo's state of mind." Critic number two writes: "His exaggerated fears of cannibalism, his horror of tattooing... and his repeated attempts to escape his kindly captors suggest that something must be wrong with Tommo." Critic number three refers to "his fear of cannibalism, which he insists upon keeping alive in himself although he is never threatened by it." Number four: "Cannibalism perfectly embodies Tommo's primitive fears, for the island has awakened the boundaryless, devouring infant within him." And number five, who refers to the illusions not of Tommo but of Melville himself: "Melville may not actually have feared cannibalism, but he seems to have been plagued by psychosomatic symptoms of tension."[12]

The only possibility not entertained by these critics is that a man isolated among known cannibals might fear for his life. What calls for explanation is the psychology of Melville's reluctance to face the realities of Typee, as evidenced in his managing to ignore cannibalism during the intermissions of his fears. Eventually, as the Typees grow importunate to impose on him what Melville terms "the hideous blemish of tattooing," he recognizes their determination to adopt him as one of them. Now he is in danger not so much of being eaten as of having to join in the eating of human flesh—a quite sufficient reason to seek escape that has also not occurred to the critics.

As it happens, just two years after the appearance of *Typee*, an account of another recent sojourn among the Marquesans was published by one William Torrey, like Melville a young sailor who jumped ship. Torrey too was held as an unwilling guest—for eighteen months. During this time he found it necessary to preserve his life by submitting to being tattooed (on the hands) and then to eating human flesh.[13]

But for some critics it is not enough to deny that Tommo is in danger. He is indicted as well for failing to appreciate the *virtues* of cannibalism. That practice, it is explained, is actually a "ritual"—than which there is no higher term of approbation in contemporary literary criticism. Cannibalism intends only the ritual "ingestion of the enemy's virtue," one critic explains. Thus we suffer from "a false understanding of cannibalism" if, like Tommo, we regard it simply as a matter of killing and eating. For when Tommo sees "first shrunken heads, and then a skeleton in a box to which cling morsels passed over by sated feeders," these "focusing images" serve to expose his inadequate view of cannibalism—an act that "is less a dietary practice than a ritual ingestion of the antagonist's virtue." The benighted Tommo, the argument continues, fails to recognize that the cannibal "is therefore mindful of the individuality of the vanquished." Indeed, the virtues of cannibalism are precisely those calculated to expose Tommo's failures of humanism: "The true difference between Tommo's and the Typees' views of cannibalism is that he considers individuality to be completely free of its vessel, and so concludes that to eat the body is to express contempt for the self: whereas they treat the body as a rich and necessary participant in the personality that is indisociably immured in its texture."[14] "So much for decadent Western dualism," one imagines Cannibal A remarking to Cannibal B as the two perform their richly integrative act.

The critics' apologies for cannibalism clash not only with common sense but also with Melville's treatment of the subject throughout *Typee*. For, far from celebrating cannibalism as ritual, Melville refers to the practice much as he does to "savages." His expressions are "many a horrid rite," "the frightful genius of native worship," and "irreclaimable cannibals." Read selectively, it is true, *Typee* can be made to yield up a defense of cannibalism as well as of savagery. Early in the book, for example, Melville dismisses the charge that the Typees trapped and ate white sailors, claiming that they ate only the flesh of their enemies (not their "slain attackers," with its implication that all Typeean battles were defensive). In the scene of discovering the human remains, though, Melville realizes that inasmuch as the severed heads before him have been hanging overhead in pots since his arrival, they cannot belong to recently killed enemy warriors as his hosts insist. "It was plain," Melville writes, "that I had seen the last relic of some unfortunate wretch, who must have been massacred on the beach by the savages, in one of those perilous trading adventures which I have before described." It is at this point that Melville—or if one prefers, Tommo— expresses the fear for his life that contemporary critics are united in dismissing.

To be sure, the critics base their apologies for cannibalism not only on Melville but also on the evidence of modern anthropology. Yet this evidence too proves to be very different from what they imagine. As Melville's discovery scene indicates, cannibalism was *not* limited to the ingestion of the enemy's virtue. One learns from anthropology, furthermore, that the Typeeans ate children as well as adults, their own tribesmen as well as enemies (and hapless strangers found on the beach). Furthermore, human flesh was eaten not only in ritual but also as part of the Typeean diet. Nor was the act of cannibalizing limited to warriors, as in some other South Sea islands. It was practiced by women and children as well as men. As for the enemies among those who were eaten, these were by no means limited to battle casualties being used in celebrations of victory: "[Cannibalistic] sacrifices occurred when victims were available at all life-crisis rites of high-status individuals, particularly death, for warfare, to break droughts, to improve harvests, and to ensure the success of constructions."[15] The permanent state of war (of which Melville was aware) applied equally to the Typees and their neighbors. It involved every man, woman, and child's fear of being taken captive, tortured, and eaten whenever ritual victims were required, which was virtually all of the time.

As to what took place at these rituals, the fragmentary details available throw a ghastly light on the apologetics of contemporary literary critics. Tortures prior to immolation could last for several days. "In cases where a victim was taken alive," a modern anthropologist reveals, "parts of his body would often be carved, cooked, and eaten before his eyes." At other times, "eyes were often eaten raw."[16] Dreadful tortures, the eating of children, a life punctuated by cannibal feasts: these are the realities of Typeean life. They make it possible to answer with some confidence the question "Who are the real cannibals?"

Literary critics have had fun with the inflated rhetoric of "degraded and benighted practices" used by nineteenth-century moralists like William Oland Bourne. Melville himself disarmed his reader by joking at the beginning of *Typee* about "cannibal banquets" and, in humorous italics, "heathenish rites and human sacrifices." By the end of the book, though, these phrases take on a deadly seriousness. In view of the narrator's discovery of human remains (and the anthropological reality behind it), the genuine shock of nineteenth-century man, albeit pompously expressed, does him more credit than the contemporary literary critic's unflappable sophistication.

To be sure, the attempt to gloss over cannibalism goes all

the way back to Montaigne. Up through the nineteenth century, though, it was possible to regard cannibalism as an anomalous, infrequently encountered, minor blot on otherwise ideal societies. Today we know—or ought to know—that cannibalism is no anomaly and is by no means the only defect of the societies in which it appears. Freud observed in *Civilization and Its Discontents* that primitive peoples are subject to "restrictions of a different kind but perhaps of greater severity than those attaching to modern civilized man." He had in mind the operations of taboo, well described by Melville and identified clearly enough in *Typee* as a system too restrictive for a freethinking Westerner to survive in. "The savage," Melville writes of the taboo, "lives in the continual observance of its dictates, which guide and control every action of his being."

Both the taboo and other restrictions among the Typees extended to their fabled sexual freedom and openness. In each family the appearance of unfettered lovemaking hinted at by Melville was, it develops, belied by the chief husband's control over sexual access to his wife by secondary husbands. The system of multiple husbands and lovers for the women, by the way, hardly supports the contention that Melville's flight from Typee was an "abandonment of loved ones." He could hardly have maintained his romantic relationship with Fayaway on Typee except as a pauper and virtual outcast in society. This is because wealth and status came from attracting subordinate husbands to share one's wife.

The psychoanalyst Abram Kardiner suggested that as a result of the chief husband's control, most Typeean males nurtured a suppressed jealousy. This found its expression in a resentment of women reflected in certain taboos and in the culture's folklore. For example, women were forbidden by taboo to enter canoes. Their genitals could render taboo any objects which they passed over. The apparently enviable sexual activity available to women was, like much else in the culture, not entirely a matter of free choice. Ritual sexual dancing followed by public sexual intercourse was regarded as a woman's "religious obligation." Similarly, Typeean children were sexually uninhibited, but a girl's introduction to sex was often by rape: an eighteenth-century traveler witnessed a girl of eight being held down by four women and made to undergo intercourse.

Melville experienced some of the coercive tendencies of Typee society, but he did not recognize the degree to which these were modulated during his stay. For he had stumbled upon a scarcity economy at a time of remission from its problem of food supply. Though there were no visible signs at the time, the Typees were actually subject to periodic famines. Soon after the islands had come under European observation some years before Melville's arrival, a famine had lasted from 1803 to 1813, wiping out an estimated two-thirds of the population. Except for the privileged few, the best the society had been able to devise in preparation for its six- and seven-year droughts was a method of storing a one or two years' breadfruit supply. There was neither any Typee agriculture (as Melville did note), nor any provision for feeding the tribe's pigs, nor means devised to harvest enough protein from the abundant ocean.

The great feasts, contributing to the impression of abundance reported by Melville and others, were actually expressions of anxiety reflecting far leaner years in the past. Similarly the resentful taboos on females reflected an accompanying belief in their responsibility for scarcity. As other early travelers reported, in order to bring rain when the breadfruit failed, a young girl was brought forth and publicly strangled to death by her brother. And during a famine in 1797 "the natives amused themselves" by administering a slight push to a starving, staggering woman and then watching as she toppled to the ground.

It is sometimes argued that the acts of the Typees and other natives occur on a small scale, whereas the depredations of Westerners, particularly venereal disease, have amounted, as one critic put it, to "genocide."[17] Yet the unfortunate ravages caused by the transmission of venereal disease from the West, aside from falling short of genocide, were entirely inadvertent. In contrast the Typees conducted "full fledged wars of extermination." In an amphibious assault on a nearby island they put to death the entire population of a rival tribe—an act of conscious, successful genocide.

One could go on. The list of misconceptions about the Typees covers most of what the critics think they know about them. Sacrificial torture, killing, and cannibalizing were normally carried out only on behalf of the "well placed," a circumstance that refutes the idea of an egalitarian society. Though material objects were not subject to theft, as Melville indicated, unbeknownst to him the theft of food was common. The Typees were most certainly a beautiful, physically robust people. But the analysis of burial remains shows a high incidence of arthritis as early in life as adolescence.

Given the increase in anthropological knowledge about the shortcomings of Typeean culture, the concurrent increase in self-delusion among literary critics calls for some explanation. In the 1970s the liberal and radical politics that had from the beginnings of *Typee* criticism been associated with cultural relativism and celebration of the primitive were adapted to the terms of contemporary politics. Melville's book came to be associated with charges of imperialist war upon and subjugation of Third World peoples. The critic who used the term *aggressor nations* meant by it "capitalist nations." The critic who found alienation in Tommo's psychology related it to "the alienation of labor in industrial society."

More up to date, another critic has refined the meaning of "exploitation" as it applies to the West in general and Tommo in particular. Without accusing Tommo of taking economic advantage of the Typees, this critic charges him with *mentally* using them for his own selfish purposes. Tommo's contrasting of his own culture to theirs is condemned as an act of "imaginative imperialism." By using the Typees in an argument, it is explained, Tommo makes himself "complicit in the [Western] brutality he claims to deplore." Thus the civilized man's habit of thought is treated as a brutal crime, whereas the primitive's actual brutalities are termed features of an "independent cultural coherence." All this, moreover, is assumed to have been "deliberately" implied by Melville.[18]

On the contrary, Melville was at once less ideological and more subversive than his recent critics imagine. Their tendency is to justify the discontents of civilization. In contrast *Typee* plunges the reader directly into the disturbing experience of those discontents. The reader subsequently accepts Melville's abrupt return to civilization, but only reluctantly. The lingering impression left by *Typee* is one of unfettered pleasure. Irate defenses of civilization in the manner of William Oland Bourne, and denunciations of it as capitalistic in the manner of the latest critics, equally violate the literary integrity of Melville's work.

Criticism properly enters the picture on a different level. Its first responsibility is to honor the literary experience, its second to relocate the frequently subversive thrust of that experience in the context of more permanent values. In times of cultural upheaval such as the 1960s these tasks come to seem particularly onerous. Criticism grows unpopular with critics themselves. Some of them claim literature's privilege of immersion in the destructive element. Still others subordinate their critical understanding to their political convictions. They prove to abandon their literary responsibilities in favor of political denunciation. On another level editors prepare texts under the broad influence of the same attitudes.

Underlying these attitudes is a cultural relativism that, while supposedly grounded in anthropologically sophisticated insight, actually rests on an anthropological double standard. Toward the primitive, a stance of nonjudgmental scientific objectivity is assumed; toward the civilized, one of subjective morality. The confident ethnocentrism of native cultures is admired, but the very right to exist of one's own culture is denied. So powerful have the imperatives of relativism grown, in fact, that not only can the norms of logic be suspended in its service, but also the cultivated sensibility that turns us away in disgust from cannibalism. For the critics of *Typee*, virtually any abandonment of values has been preferable to admitting an allegiance to civilization.

NOTES

Introduction

1. Gerald Graff, "American Criticism Left and Right," in Sacvan Bercovitch and Myra Jehlen, eds., *Ideology and Classic American Literature* (Cambridge, England, 1986), 109. Sacvan Bercovitch, *The Office of "The Scarlet Letter."* (Baltimore, 1991), 152.

2. Frederick Crews, *The Critics Bear It Away: American Fiction and the Academy* (New York, 1992), 40. Sacvan Bercovitch, "The Problem of Ideology in American Literary History," *Critical Inquiry*, Summer 1986, 638. Barbara Foley, "Subversion and Oppositionality in the Academy," *College Literature*, February 9, 1990, 68–69.

3. Jonathan Arac, "The Politics of *The Scarlet Letter*," in Bercovitch and Jehlen, *Ideology and Classic American Literature*, 258–259.

4. For Habegger and Fetterly's techniques see Chapter 5, on *The Bostonians*, in the present volume.

5. Graff, "American Criticism Left and Right," 111.

6. *American Literary Scholarship*, Annual 1978, 429, 419, 424, 422.

7. Waggoner's review was of Nina Baym, *The Shape of Hawthorne's Career* (1976); Kenneth Dauber, *Rediscovering Hawthorne* (1977); and Edgar A. Dryden, *Nathaniel Hawthorne: The Poetics of Enchantment* (1977). The review was reprinted in Waggoner's *The Presence of Hawthorne* (Baton Rouge, 1979).

8. Henry Nash Smith, "Symbol and Idea in *Virgin Land*," in *Ideology and Classic American Literature*, 28. Sacvan Bercovitch, Afterword to the same volume, 421. For an earlier Smith recantation see my *The War*

Against the Intellect: Episodes in the Decline of Discourse (Iowa City, Iowa, 1989), 93–94. For accommodationist reversals by the older critics James Cox and Charles Anderson see the chapters on *Huckleberry Finn* and *The Bostonians* in the present volume.

9. David H. Hirsch, *The Deconstruction of Literature: Criticism After Auschwitz* (Hanover, N.H., 1991), 184, 185–186. I have tried to identify critics who do not hew to the radical revisionist orthodoxy in the notes to the chapters that follow this introduction.

10. Myra Jehlen, "New World Epics: The Novel and the Middle Class in America," *Salmagundi*, Winter 1977, 67.

11. D. H. Lawrence, *Studies in Classic American Literature* (New York, 1984), 171. Perry Miller, ed., *Major Writers of America*, I, 84, quoted by Rowland A. Sherrill, *The Prophetic Melville: Experience, Transcendence, and Tragedy* (Athens, Ga., 1979), 85.

1. The Scarlet Letter

1. Anthony Trollope, "The Genius of Nathaniel Hawthorne," *North American Review*, September 1879, reprinted in Kenneth Lynn, ed., *"The Scarlet Letter": Text, Sources, Criticism* (New York, 1961), 172.

2. Trollope, "Genius of Hawthorne," 171, 172.

3. George B. Loring, "Hawthorne's *Scarlet Letter*," *Massachusetts Quarterly Review*, September 1850, reprinted in Lynn, *"The Scarlet Letter,"* 160.

4. Loring, 157.

5. For criticism from 1876 through the 1930s see Neal F. Doubleday, "Hawthorne's Hester and Feminism," PMLA, September 1939, 825.

6. Charles Child Walcutt, *"The Scarlet Letter* and Its Modern Critics," *Nineteenth-Century Fiction*, March 1953, 264.

7. From Richard H. Fogle, *Hawthorne's Fiction: The Light and the Dark*, 1952, rev. ed. 1964, in J. Donald Crowley, ed., *Nathaniel Hawthorne, A Collection of Criticism* (New York, 1975), 73. For *The Scarlet Letter* as a critique of Puritanism, see Walcutt, "*Scarlet Letter* and Modern Critics," and for examples see A. N. Kaul, *The American Vision: Actual and Ideal Society in Nineteenth-Century Fiction* (New Haven, 1963).

8. From Randall Stewart, *American Literature and Christian Doctrine* (Baton Rouge, 1958), reprinted in Sculley Bradley *et al*, eds., *The Scarlet Letter* (New York, 1961), 348; and see R. W. B. Lewis, *The American Adam* (Chicago, 1955), 112, and Fogle, *Hawthorne's Fiction*, 72. "Of all

crimes the most excusable": Fogle, 64. From Waggoner, *Hawthorne: A Critical Study* (Cambridge, Mass., 1955), reprinted in Charles Feidelson, Jr., and Paul Brodtkorb, Jr., eds., *Interpretations of American Literature* (New York, 1959), 22.

9. Darrel Abel, "Hawthorne's Hester," *College English*, 1952, reprinted in Abel, *The Moral Picturesque: Studies in Hawthorne's Fiction* (West Lafayette, Ind., 1988), 181, 188. See also Hugh N. MacLean, "Hawthorne's *Scarlet Letter*: 'The Dark Problem of This Life,'" *American Literature*, March 1955, 17.

10. Fogle, *Hawthorne's Fiction*, 64, 72.

11. Abel, "Hawthorne's Hester," 188; Marius Bewley, *The Eccentric Design: Form in the Classic American Novel* (New York, 1959), 163; Lewis, *The American Adam*, 112–113.

12. Harold Kaplan, *Democratic Humanism and American Literature* (Chicago, 1972), 138. Quentin Anderson called the act an "error" in *The Imperial Self: An Essay in American Literary and Cultural History* (New York, 1971), 83–84. David Levin, Introduction to Laurel edition of *The Scarlet Letter* (New York, 1960), 13.

13. Feidelson, *"The Scarlet Letter,"* in Roy Harvey Pearce, ed., *Hawthorne Centenary Essays* (Columbus, Ohio, 1964), 34.

14. Feidelson, "consequences": Introduction (revised from 1947) to *The Scarlet Letter* (New York, 1963), x. See also David Levin, *"The Scarlet Letter,"* in Wallace Stegner, ed., *The American Novel from James Fenimore Cooper to William Faulkner* (New York, 1965), 18; and Richard Chase, *The American Novel and Its Tradition* (Garden City, N.Y., 1957), 72. "Moral achievement": Feidelson, *"The Scarlet Letter,"* 35. See also Kaplan, *Democratic Humanism*, 137; Louise Bogan, "Nathaniel Hawthorne" (1960), in Robert Phelps and Ruth Limmer, eds., *A Poet's Alphabet: Reflections on the Literary Art and Vocation by Louise Bogan* (New York, 1970), 208. Other critics on tragedy: Robert Penn Warren, "Hawthorne Revisited: Some Remarks on Hellfiredness," *Sewanee Review*, January–March 1973, reprinted in Harold Bloom, ed., *Hester Prynne* (New York, 1990), 106; Seymour L. Gross, "'Solitude, and Love, and Anguish': The Tragic Design of *The Scarlet Letter*," *CLA Journal*, March 1960, reprinted in Sculley Bradley *et al*, eds., *The Scarlet Letter* (New York, 1962), 362; Malcolm Cowley, "Five Acts of *The Scarlet Letter*," *College English*, October 1957, reprinted in Bradley, *The Scarlet Letter*, 330. Randall Stewart is the exception in saying that Hester is *not* a tragic figure: *American Literature and Christian Doctrine*, 345.

15. Abel, "The Strong Division Lines of Nature" (1972), in *The Moral Picturesque*, 177. Austin Warren, "*The Scarlet Letter*: A Literary Exercise in Moral Theology," *Southern Review*, Winter 1965, 26, 25. For ambiguity in the characters see Kaplan, *Democratic Humanism*, 129.

16. Michael J. Colacurcio, "Footsteps of Anne Hutchinson: The Context of *The Scarlet Letter*," *ELH*, September 1972, 494.

17. Colacurcio, "'The Woman's Own Choice': Sex, Metaphor, and the Puritan 'Sources' of *The Scarlet Letter*," in *New Essays on "The Scarlet Letter"* (Cambridge, Mass., 1985), 122.

18. Evan Carton, *The Rhetoric of American Romance: Dialectic and Identity in Emerson, Dickinson, Poe, and Hawthorne* (Baltimore, 1985), 214. For the old justifications of Hester and what Darrel Abel called critical "rebukes" of Hawthorne see Abel, "Hawthorne's Hester," 181, and the exchange between Frederic I. Carpenter and Abel: "Hester the Heretic," by Carpenter, *College English*, May 1952, and Abel, "The Critic as Prosecutor," October 1952, 34. The "lone defense" was by Waggoner, *Presence of Hawthorne*, 128. Old consensus interpretations of the 1980s were: Marianna Torgovnick, *Closure in the Novel* (Princeton, N.J., 1981); Agnes McNeill Donohue, *Hawthorne: Calvin's Ironic Stepchild* (Kent, Ohio, 1985); and John P. McWilliams, Jr., *Hawthorne, Melville, and the American Character: A Looking-Glass Business* (Cambridge, Mass., 1984, 1985).

19. See summaries of the criticism by Frederick Newberry, *American Literary Scholarship: An Annual*, 1988, 21, and Louise DeSalvo, *Nathaniel Hawthorne* (Atlantic Highlands, N.J., 1987), 24.

20. DeSalvo, *Nathaniel Hawthorne*, 65. See also John Carlos Rowe, "The Internal Conflict of Romantic Narrative: Hegel's *Phenomenology* and Hawthorne's *The Scarlet Letter*," *Modern Language Notes*, 1980, 1221; Sacvan Bercovitch, "The A-Politics of Ambiguity in *The Scarlet Letter*," *New Literary History: A Journal of Theory and Interpretation*, Spring 1988, 636, 630; James M. Mellard, "Pearl and Hester: A Lacanian Reading," in David B. Kesterton, ed., *Critical Essays on Hawthorne's "The Scarlet Letter"* (Boston, 1988), reprinted in Bloom, *Hester Prynne*, 176; and Emily Miller Budick, "Sacvan Bercovitch, Stanely Cavell, and the Romance Theory of American Fiction," *PMLA*, January 1992, 87. Nina Baym complains about critical treatment of Hester, as discussed by Ross C. Murfin, *Nathaniel Hawthorne: "The Scarlet Letter"* in Murfin, ed., *The Scarlet Letter* (Boston, 1991), 220–221. The single older essay truly hard on Hester is William Bysshe Stein, *Hawthorne's Faust: A Study of the Devil's Archetype* (Gainesville, Fla., 1953). Harsh comments on her appear in MacLean,

"Hawthorne's *Scarlet Letter*," and Feidelson, *"The Scarlet Letter,"* and in transcendental readings. "Crime": Amy Schrager Lang, *Prophetic Woman: Anne Hutchinson and the Profession of Dissent in the Literature of New England* (Berkeley, 1987), 167.

21. "Self-dramatization": Lang, *Prophetic Woman*, 170. "Subtle...critique": Bercovitch, "A-Politics," 632, and see Lauren Berlant, *The Anatomy of National Fantasy: Hawthorne, Utopia, and Everyday Life* (Chicago, 1991), 142. "Spiritual pride": Lang, *Prophetic Woman*, 175, 167. "Desexed self": Larzer Ziff, *Literary Democracy: The Declaration of Cultural Independence in America* (New York, 1981, 1982), 120, and see 121. "Rigidly": Michael Davitt Bell, *The Development of American Romance: The Sacrifice of Relation* (Chicago, 1980), 178, 177. "Collaborates": Millicent Bell, "The Obliquity of Signs: *The Scarlet Letter*," *Massachusetts Review*, Spring 1982, 20. "Reflection of evil": DeSalvo, *Nathaniel Hawthorne*, 69. "Hypocrite" and "liar": Bercovitch, "A-Politics," 633, 632, 639.

22. "Tortured ambivalence": Andrew J. Scheiber, "Public Force, Private Sentiment: Hawthorne and the Gender of Politics," *American Transcendental Quarterly*, December 1988, 287 (commenting on other critics of the 1980s who take the same position). "Ambiguous toward himself": Judith Fryer, *The Faces of Eve: Women in the Nineteenth Century American Novel* (New York, 1976), reprinted in Bloom, *Hester Prynne*, 74, and see 72 for Hawthorne's supposed lack of success in this attempt. "Sublimated sexuality": Robert Shulman, *Social Criticism and Nineteenth-Century American Fictions* (Columbia, Mo., 1987), 191. "Repressed authorial anxieties," etc.: Joanne Feit Diehl, "Re-Reading *The Letter*: Hawthorne, the Fetish, and the (Family) Romance," in Murfin, ed., *The Scarlet Letter*, 243, 237, 245 (revised version of 1988 essay).

23. "Partly aware" and "qualify the impact": Shulman, *Social Criticism*, 185–191, and see Berlant, *Anatomy of National Fantasy*, 102. "Fear of disapproval": David Leverenz, "Mrs. Hawthorne's Headache: Reading *The Scarlet Letter*," *Nineteenth-Century Fiction*, March 1983, 263. "Deeply threatening": Shulman, 187. "Shocks": Colacurcio, "The Woman's Own Choice," 127; 1972 version: "Footsteps of Ann Hutchinson," 481–482. "Failure of courage": Scheiber, "Public Force," 289 (commenting on other critics, with whom he agrees).

24. Marketplace explanation: Michael T. Gilmore, *American Romanticism and the Marketplace* (Chicago, 1985), 90. Women's movement: Nina Baym, *The Scarlet Letter: A Reading* (Boston, 1986), 82. Revolutions of 1848: Larry J. Reynolds, *European Revolutions and the American Literary*

Renaissance (New Haven, 1988). "Subversive": Jonathan Arac, "The Politics of *The Scarlet Letter*," in Bercovitch, *Ideology and Classic American Literature*, 259. "Reactionary spirit": Reynolds, *European Revolutions*, 81 (Reynolds, though, does not chide Hawthorne in the manner of the other critics). "Affirmation of the state": Berlant, *Anatomy of National Fantasy*, 157, and see 168 for Berlant's reference to "the state semiotic apparatus." "Domination and subjection": Elizabeth Aycock Hoffman, "Political Power in *The Scarlet Letter*," *American Transcendental Quarterly*, March 1990, 15, 14.

25. "Linguistic imprecision": David Van Leer, "Hester's Labyrinth: Transcendental Rhetoric in Puritan Boston," in Colacurcio, ed., *New Essays*, 70. "Confusing ambivalence": Mary Suzanne Schriber, *Gender and the Writer's Imagination: From Cooper to Wharton* (Lexington, Ky., 1987), 60. "Incoherent": Van Leer, "Hester's Labyrinth," 87. "Cavils and contradictions": Leverenz, "Mrs. Hawthorne's Headache," 268, and see, on "contradictions," Bercovitch, *The Office of "The Scarlet Letter"* (Baltimore, 1991), 157, and Zelda Bronstein, "The Parabolic Ploys of *The Scarlet Letter*," *American Quarterly*, Summer 1987, 197. "Impedes": Lang, *Prophetic Woman*, 175. "Unconscionable": Van Leer, 67. "Punitive plotting": Leverenz, 273.

26. "Fearful cruelty" and "a Dimmesdale": Leverenz, "Mrs. Hawthorne's Headache," 271. "Ideological limitations": Elizabeth Hoffman, "Political Power," 15. "Abdication" and "scaffold": Kenneth Dauber, *Rediscovering Hawthorne* (Princeton, N.J., 1977), 116. "Fatalistic alliance": Leverenz, "Mrs. Hawthorne's Headache," 267–268; and, for a similar prison comparison see Shulman, *Social Criticism*, 188. For resentments among older critics see David Levin, "Introduction"; Daniel Hoffman, *Form and Fable in American Fiction* (New York, 1965); and Leo Marx, Foreword, *The Scarlet Letter* (New York, 1959).

27. "Stripping her" and "condemns her": Diehl, "Re-Reading *The Letter*," 246. "He claims": Schriber, *Gender and the Writer's Imagination*, 53. DeSalvo summarizes similar approaches in *Nathaniel Hawthorne*, 72.

28. Arac, "Politics of *Scarlet Letter*," 259. Compare Bercovitch, "A-Politics," 650, on Hester: "It is as though under pressure of her resistance the letter were slipping out of his control."

29. Murfin, "Introduction: The Biographical and Historical Background," in *The Scarlet Letter*, 5.

30. On contemporary Puritan heroines see David Reynolds, *Faith in*

Fiction: The Emergence of Religious Literature in America (Cambridge, Mass., 1981), 106.

31. Sophia Hawthorne to Mary Mann, February 12, 1850, cited by Richard H. Millington, *Practicing Romance: Narrative Form and Cultural Engagement in Hawthorne's Fiction* (Princeton, N.J., 1992), 98.

32. Chase, *The American Novel*, 73, 72. See also Nina Baym, *The Shape of Hawthorne's Career* (Ithaca, N.Y., 1976), 141. (Baym came to see Puritan society as less representative in *The Scarlet Letter: A Reading* (1986), 63.)

2. Moby-Dick

1. F. O. Matthiessen, *American Renaissance: Art and Expression in the Age of Emerson and Whitman* (New York, 1941), 445, 437, 405.

2. Henry Nash Smith, "The Image of Society in *Moby-Dick*," in Tyrus Hillway, ed., *Moby-Dick: Centennial Essays* (Dallas, 1953), 60.

3. Matthiessen, *American Renaissance*, 459.

4. *Ibid.*, 401.

5. Smith, "Image of Society," 65–66.

6. *Ibid.*, 75.

7. Matthiessen, *American Renaissance*, ix.

8. Charles H. Foster, "Something in Emblems: A Reinterpretation of *Moby-Dick*," *New England Quarterly*, March 1961, 534.

9. Alan Heimert, "*Moby-Dick* and American Political Symbolism," *American Quarterly*, April 1963, 529.

10. *Ibid.*, 532, 515, 504.

11. *Ibid.*, 534; Foster, "Something in Emblems," 35.

12. Leo Marx, *The Machine in the Garden: Technology and the Pastoral Ideal in America* (New York, 1964), 298.

13. Milton R. Stern, "*Moby Dick*, Millennial Attitudes, and Politics," *Emerson Society Quarterly* 54 (1969), 53, 54.

14. Marx, *Machine*, 300n.

15. Stern, "Millennial Attitudes," 60.

16. Elizabeth Schultz, "*Moby-Dick*: The Little Lower Layers," *North American Review*, December 1988, 54.

17. *Ibid.*, 54, 55.

18. See Steven T. Katz, "The Pequot War Reconsidered," *New England Quarterly*, June 1991, 206–224. For Melville's sources of information

about the Pequots see the edition of *Moby-Dick* edited by Luther S. Mansfield and Howard P. Vincent (New York, 1952), 633.

19. Schultz, *"Moby-Dick,"* 56, 57.

20. Carolyn L. Karcher, *Shadow Over the Promised Land: Slavery, Race, and Violence in Melville's America* (Baton Rouge, 1980), ix, x.

21. Robert Milder, "Melville" in *American Literary Scholarship: 1983*, 61.

22. Richard Chase, *Herman Melville: A Critical Study* (New York, 1949), 101.

23. Chase is cited by Marius Bewley in *The Eccentric Design: Form in the Classic American Novel* (New York, 1959), 205, as expressing a consensus agreed on by "nearly all critics," including Henry Bamford Parkes and Newton Arvin.

24. That is, the *Iliad* and the *Odyssey, Beowulf,* and the *Lusiads.* See John P. McWilliams, Jr., *The American Epic: Transforming a Genre, 1770–1860* (New York, 1989), 190ff.

25. Philip Gleason, *"Moby-Dick*: Meditation for Democracy," *Personalist*, Autumn 1963, 499; James B. Hall, *"Moby Dick*: Parable of a Dying System," *Western Review*, Spring 1950, 225, 226.

26. "Fate of poor": Michael Paul Rogin, *Subversive Genealogy: The Politics and Art of Herman Melville* (New York, 1983), 106; "exposing essence": Bruce Franklin, "Herman Melville: Artist of the Worker's World," in Norman Rudich, ed., *Weapons of Criticism: Marxism in America and the Literary Tradition* (Palo Alto, 1976), 289; "outright condemnation": Paul Royster, "Melville's Economy of Language," in Bercovitch, *Ideology and Classic American Literature,* 313.

27. "Capitalist expansion": Rogin, *Subversive Genealogy*, 109; "industrial capitalism": Robert K. Martin, *Hero, Captain, and Stranger: Male Friendship, Social Critique, and Literary Form in the Sea Novels of Herman Melville* (Chapel Hill, 1986), 84; "capitalist appropriation" and "disappointed fetishizer": Rogin, *Subversive Genealogy*, 115, 126; "class conflict": Martin, *Hero, Captain, and Stranger*, 87, quoting Hall's 1952 Marxist essay; "proletarian crew": Carl Oglesby, "Melville, or Water Consciousness and Its Madness: A Fragment from a Work-in-Progress," *TriQuarterly*, Winter/ Spring 1972, 127. See also Rogin, *Subversive Genealogy*, 114 ("a multiracial proletariat"); Franklin, "Herman Melville," 296 ("workers"); Ziff, *Literary Democracy*, 271 (Melville's "proletarian concern" as a writer); Royster, "Melville's Economy of Language," 314 ("rhetoric of labor"); Rogin, *Subversive Genealogy*, 106 "class conflict"—in a slightly different context); also on class: Royster, "Melville's Economy of Language," 314, and Russell

J. Reising, *The Unusable Past: Theory and the Study of American Literature* (New York, 1986), 97. "Death of the Pequod": Hall, "Parable of a Dying System," 225.

28. Heimert, *"Moby-Dick,"* 532; Marx, *Machine*, 319.

29. "Annihilation": John P. McWilliams, Jr., *Hawthorne, Melville, and the American Character: A Looking-Glass Business* (New York, 1984), 159; Richard Slotkin, *Regeneration Through Violence: The Mythology of the American Frontier, 1600–1860* (Middletown, Conn., 1973), 550.

30. Rogin, *Subversive Genealogy*, 121, 123, 125, 126, 137, 141–142.

31. Martin, *Hero, Captain, and Stranger*, 88–89. Karcher, *Shadow over the Promised Land*, 77. Other critics who assume an inevitable apocalypse: Edward S. Grejda, *The Common Continent of Men: Racial Equality in the Writings of Herman Melville* (Port Washington, N.Y., 1974); David Leverenz, *Manhood and the American Renaissance* (Ithaca, N.Y., 1989); Wai-Chee Dimock, *Empire for Liberty: Melville and the Poetics of Individualism* (Princeton, N.J., 1989); James Duban, *Melville's Major Fiction: Politics, Theology, and Imagination* (De Kalb, Ill., 1983); and Carolyn Porter, "Call Me Ishmael, or How to Make Double-Talk Speak," in Richard Brodhead, ed., *New Essays on Moby-Dick* (New York, 1986).

32. "Come to grief": Oglesby, "Melville," 126; "unrepentant republic": Duban, *Melville's Major Fiction*, 83; "tragic illusion": Oglesby, "Melville," 124; "Babylon": Michael T. Gilmore, "Melville's Apocalypse: American Millennialism and *Moby-Dick*," *ESQ: A Journal of the American Renaissance*, 3rd Quarter 1975, 161, 159. And see Rogin, *Subversive Genealogy*, 106, on the hollow "republican ideals" of America.

33. Michael Boughn, "Eros and Identity in *Moby-Dick*," *American Transcendental Quarterly*, No. 3, 1987, 189; Marx, *Machine*, 296; "if we can survive": Donald E. Pease, "Melville and Cultural Persuasion," in Bercovitch, *Ideology and Classic American Literature*, 415; "logocentrism": William V. Spanos, "The 'Nameless Horror': The Errant Art of Herman Melville and Charles Hewitt," *Boundary*, Fall 1980, 130.

34. Critics who have pointed out the epic tradition and raised other objections to apocalyptic, anti-American readings include Gleason, *"Moby-Dick,"* 514, and McWilliams, *American Epic*, 212.

35. Marx, *Machine*, 298. "Integrate into . . . the money system": David Simpson, "Herman Melville: Chasing the Whale" (1982) in Harold Bloom, ed., *Herman Melville's Moby-Dick* (New York, 1986), 61. Not "part of the system": Royster, "Melville's Economy of Language," 317.

36. *Moby-Dick*, Chapter 37, cited by Smith, "Image of Society," 60.

37. Marx, *Machine*, 306; Schultz, *"Moby-Dick,"* 56. For a more balanced approach see Stephen C. Ausband, "The Whale and the Machine: An Approach to *Moby-Dick," American Literature*, May 1975, 200.

38. "Patriarchal search": Martin, *Hero, Captain, and Stranger*, 85; "expansionist voyage": Duban, *Melville's Major Fiction*, 90; the third critic is Rogin, *Subversive Genealogy*, 138 (and compare Spanos, "The 'Nameless Horror,'" 131); "subduing nature": Martin, *Hero, Captain, and Stranger*, 85.

39. Holding a low opinion of Starbuck is not new. See Robert Zoellner, *The Salt-Sea Mastodon: A Reading of Moby-Dick* (Berkeley, 1973), 114, and Daniel Hoffman, *Form and Fable in American Fiction* (New York, 1961, 1965), 269. In sympathy with Starbuck is, among others, Chase, *Herman Melville*, 108. "Most admirable": Gleason, *"Moby-Dick,"* 505; "accessory": Joyce Sparer Adler, *War in Melville's Imagination* (New York, 1981), 70; "manufactured man": Marx, *Machine*, 313; "sorrowing liberalism": Oglesby, "Melville," 135; "tragedy": Dimock, *Empire for Liberty*, 121. More nuanced on Starbuck are Wynn M. Goering, " 'To Obey, Rebelling': The Quaker Dilemma in *Moby-Dick," New England Quarterly*, December 1981, 519–538, and T. Walter Herbert, Jr., *Moby-Dick and Calvinism: A World Dismantled* (New Brunswick, N.J., 1977), 153.

40. Adler, *War in Melville's Imagination*, 71. For *Moby-Dick* as a pacifist tract see Karcher, *Shadow over the Promised Land*, and Martin, *Hero, Captain, and Stranger*. Earlier, balanced assessments of Queequeg include Hoffman, *Form and Fable*; Edwin Fussell, *Frontier: American Literature and the American West* (Princeton, N.J., 1965), and as with Starbuck, Herbert, *Moby-Dick and Calvinism*.

41. See Henry Nash Smith, *Democracy and the Novel: Popular Resistance to Classic American Writers* (New York, 1978), 51 and note 26.

42. Larry J. Reynolds, *European Revolutions and the American Literary Renaissance* (New Haven, 1988), 118, 121. For an earlier refutation of the Melville-as-radical thesis see Hershel Parker, "Melville and Politics: A Scrutiny of the Political Milieux of Herman Melville's Life and Works," Ph.D. dissertation, Northwestern University, 1963, especially 202.

43. Larry J. Reynolds, "Kings and Commoners in *Moby-Dick," Studies in the Novel*, Summer 1980, 101, 102.

44. Recognizing Ahab's attraction are Karcher, *Shadow over the Promised Land*, 91n, and Pease, "Melville and Cultural Persuasion," 386, where Ahab is championed.

45. " 'Canon,' Theme, and Code," in Virgil Nemoianu and Robert

Royal, eds., *The Hospitable Canon: Essays on Literary Play, Scholarly Choice, and Popular Pressures* (Amsterdam, 1991), 209.

46. Jeremy Ingalls, "The Epic Tradition; a Commentary," *East-West Review* (Kyoto, Doshisha University Press), Spring 1964, 45.

47. For interpretations along these lines see Chase, *Herman Melville*, and Smith, *Democracy and the Novel*, especially 45–46.

3. Billy Budd

1. Harrison Hayford and Merton Sealts, Jr., Editors' Introduction, *Billy Budd, Sailor (An Inside Narrative)* (Chicago, 1962), 8.

2. For the "acceptance" reading see E. L. Grant Watson, "Melville's Testament of Acceptance" (1933), reprinted in Howard P. Vincent, *Twentieth Century Interpretations of Billy Budd* (Englewood Cliffs, N.J., 1971); for "resistance" see Phil Withim, "*Billy Budd*: Testament of Resistance," *Modern Language Quarterly* XX (1959); "respect necessity" is from Matthiessen, *American Renaissance*, 510; "harsh...acceptance": Herbert Weisinger and Adrian J. Jaffe, "Billy and Oedipus," (1960), reprinted in William T. Stafford, ed., *Melville's Billy Budd and the Critics* (San Francisco, 1961), 150.

3. Lawrence Thompson, *Melville's Quarrel with God* (Princeton, N.J., 1952), 360; for disagreement among ironists see Hayford and Sealts, Editors' Introduction, 27.

4. *Ibid.*, 26; Geraldine Murphy calls the "resistance" reading "critical orthodoxy by the late '60s" in "The Politics of Reading *Billy Budd*," *American Literary History*, Summer 1989, 376.

5. E. H. Rosenberry, "The Problem of *Billy Budd*," *PMLA* 80 (1965), 489–498.

6. Melville, *White Jacket, or The World in a Man-of-War* (New York, 1979), 222; also cited by Norman Holmes Pearson, "*Billy Budd*: The King's Yarn," *American Quarterly* 3 (1951), 103.

7. William James, *The Naval History of Great Britain* (1860), II, 64–65, also cited in Olive L. Fite, "The Interpretation of *Billy Budd*," Ph.D. dissertation, University of Michigan, 1956. See C. B. Ives, "*Billy Budd* and the Articles of War," *American Literature* 34 (March 1962), regarding punishments for striking an officer.

8. Stanton Garner, "Fraud as Fact in Herman Melville's *Billy Budd*," *San Jose Studies* 4 (1978), 103.

9. This is, in fact, what Richard H. Weisberg argues. See Weisberg, *The Failure of the Word: The Protagonist as Lawyer in Modern Fiction* (New Haven, 1984).

10. Milton R. Stern, Introduction to *Billy Budd, Sailor (An Inside Narrative)* (Indianapolis, 1975), xliv.

11. Lionel Trilling, *The Middle of the Journey* (New York, 1947), 155; subsequent quotations are from 155–159. George Monteiro thinks Trilling rejects Maxim, whom I take, on the contrary, to echo the thesis of Trilling's *The Liberal Imagination*; see Monteiro, "The Doubloon: Trilling's Melville Problem," *Canadian Review of American Studies* 17 (1986), 27–34.

12. Roland A. Duerksen, "The Deep Quandary in *Billy Budd*," *New England Quarterly* 41 (1968), 51; Duerksen quotes "a call to rebellion" from John Bernstein, *Pacifism and Rebellion in the Writings of Herman Melville* (The Hague, 1964). For "political evil" and "the people" see Ray B. Browne, "*Billy Budd*: Gospel of Democracy," *Nineteenth-Century Fiction* 4 (1964), 337, 322.

13. For Vere as "organization man" see Charles Mitchell, "Melville and the Spurious Truth of Legalism," *Centennial Review of Arts and Sciences* 12 (1966), 126; for Vere as "upholder of the 'status quo,'" Duerksen, "Deep Quandary," 54; as rigid authoritarian, Kingsley Widmer, *The Ways of Nihilism: A Study of Herman Melville's Short Novels* (Los Angeles, 1970), 7.

The idea that *Billy Budd* is an imperfect story is offered by Walter L. Reed, "The Measured Forms of Captain Vere," *Modern Fiction Studies* 23 (1979), 227–235; for *Billy Budd* as a meaningless story see Peter A. Obuchowsky, "*Billy Budd* and the Failure of Art," *Studies in Fiction* 15 (1978), 448; as Rorschach test by which the reader "exposes his own nature" see Jon M. Kinnamon, "*Billy Budd*: Political Philosophies in a Sea of Thought," *Arizona Quarterly* 26 (1970), 172; also Barbara Johnson, "Melville's Fist: The Execution of Billy Budd," *Studies in Romanticism* 18 (1979), 567–599; R. Evan Davis, "An Allegory of America in Melville's *Billy Budd*," *Journal of Narrative Technique* 14/3 (1984), 174; and Robert Milder, in Emory Elliott *et al*, eds., *Columbia Literary History of the United States* (New York, 1988), 446.

14. Johnson, "Melville's Fist," 588–589. For Vere as "martinet" see William Bysshe Stein, "*Billy Budd*: The Nightmare of History," *Criticism* 3 (1961), 243; as "persecutor," Mitchell, "Spurious Truth," 119, 126; as "monomaniac" and "sado-masochistic," Eric Mottram, "Orpheus and Measured Forms: Law, Madness and Reticence in Melville," and as "primi-

tively" inspired, C. N. Manlove, "An Organic Hesitancy: Theme and Style in *Billy Budd*," both in Faith Pullin, ed., *New Perspectives on Melville* (Kent, Ohio, 1978), 250, 284; as "monomaniac," Mottram, "Orpheus and Measured Forms," 250.

For Vere's speech as "wicked...rhetoric" see William H. Shurr, *The Mystery of Iniquity: Melville as Poet, 1857–1871* (Lexington, Ky., 1972), 251; Shurr is quoted and approved by Bruce Franklin, "From Empire to Empire: *Billy Budd, Sailor*," in A. Robert Lee, ed., *Herman Melville: Reassessments* (New York, 1984), 205; for Vere as "war criminal," and "commandant" see Widmer, *Ways of Nihilism*, 38, 32–33.

15. See Eric Henderson, "Vices of the Intellect in *Billy Budd*," *English Studies in Canada* 11 (1985), 40; Johnson, "Melville's Fist," 586; Adler, *War in Melville's Imagination*, 185; Weisberg, *Failure of the Word*, 161; Brook Thomas, "The Legal Fictions of Herman Melville and Lemuel Shaw," *Critical Inquiry* 11 (1984), 43; Franklin, "From Empire to Empire," 201. Vere as Claggart is foreshadowed by Leonard Casper, "The Case Against Captain Vere," *Perspective* 5 (1952), 150.

16. For *Billy Budd* as class conflict see Brook Thomas, "*Billy Budd* and the Judgment of Silence," *Bucknell Review* 27 (1982), 66; and Franklin, "From Empire to Empire," 215; for social responsibility of Vere's class, Christopher S. Durer, "Captain Vere and Upper-Class Mores in *Billy Budd*," *Studies in Short Fiction* 19 (1982), 15; and see Durer on the "conflict between Billy the commoner and...upper-class values," 11; for Vere as part of a "bankrupt moral system" see conclusion of Weisberg, *Failure of the Word*; as part of a "military state," Rogin, *Subversive Genealogy*, 309; "police power": Robert Shulman, "*Billy Budd*: Identity, Ideology and Power," in *Social Criticism and Nineteenth Century American Fiction* (Columbia, Mo., 1987), 68; "war machine," Adler, *War in Melville's Imagination*, 163.

17. For "Bellipotent" as "apt" name see Franklin, "From Empire to Empire," 201; as "American" ship, Rogin, *Subversive Genealogy*, 308; Nazi rallies, etc., Franklin, "From Empire to Empire," 214.

18. Stephen Vizincenzy, "Engineers of a Sham: How Literature Lies about Power," *Harper's Magazine* (May–June 1972), 73.

19. Franklin, "From Empire to Empire," 201.

20. Other critics politically troubled by assigning guilt to Vere include Rogin, *Subversive Genealogy*; Julian Markels, "The Liberal Bombast of *Billy Budd*," *Essays in Arts and Sciences* XV (1986), 43–58; and Widmer, *Ways of Nihilism*, 34.

21. Thomas, "*Billy Budd* and Silence," 57.

22. For Carpenter's argument see "Melville: The World in a Man-of-War," *University of Kansas City Review* 19 (Summer 1953), 257–264.

23. Compare Richard Chase, "Dissent on *Billy Budd*," *Partisan Review* 15 (1948), 1218.

4. Huckleberry Finn

1. On the character Jim and racism see Richard K. Barksdale, "History, Slavery, and Thematic Irony in *Huckleberry Finn*," *Mark Twain Journal* ["Black Writers on *Adventures of Huckleberry Finn* One Hundred Years Later," guest ed. Thadious M. Davis] 22 (Fall 1984), 19. Cf. Frederick Woodward and Donnarae MacCann, "*Huckleberry Finn* and the Traditions of Blackface Minstrelsy," and Donald B. Gibson, "Mark Twain's Jim in the Classroom," both in Donnarae MacCann and Gloria Woodward, eds., *The Black American in Books for Children: Readings in Racism* (Metuchen, N.J., 1985), 75–109; Arnold Rampersad, "*Adventures of Huckleberry Finn* and Afro-American Literature," *Mark Twain Journal* 22 (Fall 1984), 51; and Louis J. Budd, *Mark Twain: Social Philosopher* (Bloomington, Ind., 1962), 103.

2. "Noble grandeur...pettiness of men" is Lionel Trilling's phrase ["An Introduction to *Huckleberry Finn*"] in Richard Lettis, Robert F. McDonnell, and William E. Morris, eds., *Huck Finn and His Critics* (New York, 1962), 323. Eliot is quoted in Charles A. Norton, *Writing Tom Sawyer: The Adventures of a Classic* (Jefferson, N.C., 1983), 330.

3. Leo Marx, "Mr. Eliot, Mr. Trilling, and *Huckleberry Finn*," *American Scholar* 22 (1953), 92–93.

4. "Failure of nerve": *ibid.*, 97; Marx taxes Eliot and Trilling with taking too "lightly" the last adventure, 89.

5. Eliot as "extravagant": *ibid.*, 89; restoration of 1930s-style leftist criticism, 93; Marx's second account, "raft as symbolic locus," etc., 89–90.

6. Huck's credo, *ibid.*, 87; "climactic moment," 96; "uncertain...mode of travelling," 95.

7. Henry Nash Smith, Introduction to *Adventures of Huckleberry Finn* (Cambridge, Mass., 1958), xxii–xxiii.

8. For Jim's escape as the overt action of *Huckleberry Finn*, see *ibid.*, xv; as the "theme at the novel's center," Marx, "Mr. Eliot...," 89; Huck's "stature," *ibid.*, 87; on Huck's inability to understand the proposition,

Notes

'Slavery is wrong,' Smith, Introduction, xxii; and cf. Alan Trachtenberg, "The Form of Freedom in *The Adventures of Huckleberry Finn*," *Southern Review* 6 (1970), 954–971, for a denial that Huck holds any positive idea of freedom.

9. Huck's decision to "light out" as social critique, and the characterization of 1950s critics are both from Kenneth S. Lynn, "Welcome Back from the Raft, Huck, Honey," *American Scholar* 46 (1977), 346, 345.

10. Huck's ordeal as exposure of hypocrisy: Marx, "Mr. Eliot...," 85; "shabby morality": 90.

11. For Pap Finn, *et al* treated as overtly vicious, see Millicent Bell, "*Huckleberry Finn*: Journey Without End," *Virginia Quarterly Review* 58 (1982), 258; cf. Carey Wall, "The Boomerang of Slavery: The Child, The Aristocrat, and Hidden White Identity in *Huckleberry Finn*," *Southern Studies* 21 (1982), 215, where Pap represents "aristocracy" as well as the community in general. For critical disdain of Tom Sawyer see Judith Fetterly, "Disenchantment: Tom Sawyer in *Huckleberry Finn*," *PMLA* 87 (1972), 69–74, and "The Sanctioned Rebel," *Studies in the Novel* 3 (1971), 293–304; George C. Carrington, Jr., "Farce and *Huckleberry Finn*," in Robert Sattelmeyer and J. Donald Crowley, eds., *One Hundred Years of Huckleberry Finn: The Boy, His Book, and American Culture, Centennial Essays* (Columbia, Mo., 1985), 228; cf. Michael J. Hoffman, "Huck's Ironic Circle," *Georgia Review* 23 (1969), 312; M. J. Sidnell, "Huck and Jim: Their Abortive Freedom Ride," *Cambridge Quarterly* (2/1967), 203–211.

12. See Chadwick Hansen, "The Character of Jim and the Ending of *Huckleberry Finn*," *Massachusetts Review* 5 (1963), 59, with reference to Mark Twain's use of "depraved." Cf. Paul Taylor, "*Huckleberry Finn*: The Education of a Young Capitalist," in Sattelmeyer, *One Hundred Years of Huckleberry Finn*, 342.

13. Forrest G. Robinson, *In Bad Faith: The Dynamics of Deception in Mark Twain's America* (Cambridge, Mass., 1986), 208. Robinson's critique was anticipated by Richard Gollin and Rita Gollin, "*Huckleberry Finn* and the Time of the Evasion," *Modern Language Studies* 9 (1979), 11; Carrington, in "Farce and *Huckleberry Finn*," 225, says he took Huck to task in 1976.

14. Marx, "Mr. Eliot...," 91.

15. Ordinary folk as the "only possible authorities": Kaplan, *Democratic Humanism*, 249; cf. Mera J. Flaumenhaft, "Housebound or Floating Free: The American Home in *Huckleberry Finn*," *St. John's Review*, Summer 1985, 47–52. As "fundamentally decent people": Lynn, *Mark Twain and*

Southwestern Humor (Boston, 1959), 218; cf. Everett Carter, "The Modernist Ordeal of Huckleberry Finn," *Studies in American Fiction* 13, Autumn 1985, 171; and John Fraser, "In Defense of Culture: *Huckleberry Finn*," *Oxford Review* 6 (1967), 19. These are among the few critics who did not join the consensus. Mark Twain's comment on slavery is from his autobiography, *Life As I Find It*, ed. by Charles Neider (Garden City, N.Y., 1961), 33; cited by Gollin and Gollin, "Time of Evasion," 9. Cf. Arthur G. Pettit, *Mark Twain and the South* (Lexington, Ky., 1974), for Mark Twain's shifting views on this question.

16. Michael Egan, *Mark Twain's Huckleberry Finn: Race, Class and Society* (Sussex, England, 1977), 65; Alfred J. Levy, "The Dramatic Integrity of Huck Finn," *Ball State University Forum* 20 (1979), 34.

17. Marx, "Mr. Eliot...," 90. James M. Cox, *Mark Twain: The Fate of Humor*, (Princeton, N.J., 1966), 174.

18. Henry Nash Smith, "Guilt and Innocence in Mark Twain's Later Fiction," in his *Democracy and the Novel*, 116; cf. on the speech, William R. Manierre, "No Money for to Buy the Outfit: *Huckleberry Finn* Again," *Modern Fiction Studies* 10 (1964), 343, and Janet Holmgren McKay, *Narration and Discourse in American Realistic Fiction* (Philadelphia, 1982), 159–160. And on Mark Twain's adoption of "the sentimental formula of 19th century boys' books," cf. Carter, "Modernist Ordeal."

19. (Though not in the fearful way Marx supposed.) Santayana's comment is from "The Genteel Tradition," in Norman Henfrey, ed., *Selected Critical Writings of George Santayana* (Cambridge, England, 1968) II, 97. "High points," "complacency," and "intense self-righteousness": Smith, *Democracy and the Novel*, 112.

20. William Van O'Connor, "Why *Huckleberry Finn* Is Not the Great American Novel," in Lettis, *Huck Finn and His Critics*, 379–383.

21. "Innate dignity": Budd, *Social Philosopher*, 103; Jim as transcending his status: Hansen, "Character of Jim," 49, and cf. Thomas Weaver and Merline A. Weaver, "Mark Twain's Jim: Identity as an Index to Cultural Attitudes," *American Literary Realism* 13 (1980), 19–30, for successive treatments of Jim; as "figure from...WPA mural," J. C. Furnas, "The Crowded Raft: *Huckleberry Finn* and Its Critics," *American Scholar* 54 (1985), 520. Hoffman, "Huck's Ironic Circle," 318, 316.

22. "Evidence of Jim's humanity": Charles H. Nichols, "'A True Book— with Some Stretchers': Huck Finn Today"; as "elevated in stature," "set apart," "at the mercy of...arbitrary cruelties": David L. Smith, "Huck, Jim and American Racial Discourse"—both in *Mark Twain Journal* 22 (Fall

1984) 15 and 9, 10 respectively. Cf., in the same volume, Rampersad, "Adventures," 51: Mark Twain went further than all but one black writer of the nineteenth century in repudiating "white claims to superiority." But cf. Rhett S. Jones, "Nigger and Knowledge: White Double-Consciousness in *Adventures of Huckleberry Finn*," as the sole dissenter in the special issue. Jim as "symbol of humanity": Ralph Ellison, *Shadow and Act* (New York, 1964), 31–32 (see 50 for how Jim is demeaned).

23. On the parallel with Reconstruction see Neil Schmitz, "Twain, *Huckleberry Finn*, and the Reconstruction," *American Studies* 12 (1971), 59–67; "ambivalent": *ibid.*, 64; cf. Gollin and Gollin, "Time of Evasion," 9.

24. Walter Blair, *Mark Twain and Huck Finn* (Berkeley, 1962), 143. Cf. Woodward and McCann, *Black American in Books for Children*, 77.

25. Mark Twain as influenced by "the temper of the age": Schmitz, "Twain...and the Reconstruction," 66; see Schmitz also for interpretations of *Huckleberry Finn* as "ironic allegory"; Spencer Brown, *"Huckleberry Finn* for Our Time: A Rereading of the Concluding Chapters," *Michigan Quarterly Review* VI (1967), 44; Gollin and Gollin, "Time of Evasion."

26. Trachtenberg, "Form of Freedom," 956.

27. Marx, "Mr. Eliot...," 93.

28. Huck's relationship with Jim as unable to "counteract the slaveholding psychology": Wall, "Boomerang of Slavery," 218; *Huckleberry Finn* as "failure": Robinson, *In Bad Faith*, 216.

29. "Murder in Jim's heart": Schmitz, "Twain...and the Reconstruction," 135; see Tom Quirk, "The Legend of Noah and the Voyage of Huckleberry Finn," *Mark Twain Journal* 21 (3/1983), 22, for information that Mark Twain considered the possibility of Jim being lynched.

30. Roy Harvey Pearce, "Yours Truly, Huck Finn," in Sattelmeyer, *One Hundred Years of Huckleberry Finn*, 323.

31. "Contradiction between...whole self and the market society," "sickening disease," etc.: Robert Shulman, "Fathers, Brothers, and 'the Diseased': The Family, Individualism, and American Society in *Huck Finn*"; and Huck as avoiding "robber capitalist" temptation, Taylor, "Young Capitalist"—both in Sattelmeyer, *One Hundred Years of Huckleberry Finn*, 329, 333, and 353, respectively. Cf. Carter, "Modernist Ordeal," 169.

32. Reising, *Unusable Past*, 160. Tim William Machan, "The Symbolic Narrative of *Huckleberry Finn*," *Arizona Quarterly* 42 (Summer 1986), 131–140, is one of the few recent symbolic readings.

33. Schmitz, "Twain...and the Reconstruction," 60. See also Fritz Oelschlager, "'Gwyne to Git Hung': The Conclusion of *Huckleberry Finn*," in Sattelmeyer, *One Hundred Years of Huckleberry Finn*, 121.

34. *Huckleberry Finn* as beginning "after the *fact* of the Civil War": Cox, *Fate of Humor*, 175 (his italics); Cox, "A Hard Book to Take," in Sattelmeyer, *One Hundred Years of Huckleberry Finn*, 397, 399–400.

35. Pearce, "Yours Truly, Huck Finn," 324. And cf. Robinson, *In Bad Faith*, 241.

36. *Ibid.*, 128, 130–131, 137, 171, 180; cf. Oelschlager, "Gwyne to Git Hung," 119.

37. "Huck's conclusion regarding slavery": Smith, "Huck, Jim and American Racial Discourse"; *Huckleberry Finn* as reaffirming "the values of our democratic faith": Nichols, "A True Book," 9 and 14.

38. "Tawdry nature" of Mississippi Valley culture: Marx, "Mr. Eliot...," 90. "Trivially vicious world": Sidnell, "Huck and Jim," 211; cf. David F. Burg, "Another View of *Huckleberry Finn*," *Nineteenth-Century Fiction* 29 (12/1974), 300. Accepting "the continuation of racism...into the present": Reising, *Unusable Past*, 159.

39. Weaver and Weaver, "Mark Twain's Jim," 28; cf. Reising, *Unusable Past*, 158.

40. Exceptions to this include Carter, "Modernist Ordeal"; Flaumenhaft, "Housebound or Floating Free"; Kaplan, *Democratic Humanism*; Levy, "Dramatic Integrity"; and Burton Raffel, "Mark Twain's View of *Huckleberry Finn*," *Ball State University Forum* 24 (1983), 28–37.

41. James L. Johnson, *Mark Twain and the Limits of Power: Emerson's God in Ruins* (Knoxville, Tenn., 1982), 117.

42. Johnson, *ibid.*, 114.

5. *The Bostonians*

1. Henry James to Edmund Gosse, August 25, 1915, *Selected Letters of Henry James to Edmund Gosse, 1882–1915* (Baton Rouge, 1988), 314.

2. Richard Nicholas Foley, *Criticism in American Periodicals of the Works of Henry James From 1866 to 1916*, Ph.D. dissertation, Catholic University of America, 1944, 39–41. Oscar Cargill had it that James's contemporaries "were not educated up to" reading *The Bostonians*, and contrasts his opinion to that of Philip Rahv "and others" who ascribe the rejection to more purely political causes. *The Novels of Henry James* (New York, 1961), 133.

3. Irving Howe, Introduction to *The Bostonians* (New York, 1956), xix, xvi–xvii. Philip Rahv, Introduction to *The Bostonians* (New York, 1945), viii.

4. Lionel Trilling, "*The Bostonians*," in *The Opposing Self* (New York, 1955), 97–98.

5. Judith Fetterly, *The Resisting Reader: A Feminist Approach to American Literature* (Bloomington, Ind., 1978), 110.

6. *Ibid.*, 118. Cargill, *Novels*, 137. William McMurray, "Pragmatic Realism in *The Bostonians*" (1962) in Tony Tanner, ed., *Henry James: Modern Judgments* (Nashville, 1970), 161, 164. Compare Edmund Wilson on Olive as "horrid" (Cargill, 144n) with F. O. Matthiessen's more sympathetic response in *The American Novels and Stories of Henry James* (New York, 1956), Introduction, xix–xx; Frederick Dupee's sympathy, *Henry James* (Garden City, N.Y., 1951), 153; and the neutral Bruce R. McElderry, *Henry James* (New Haven, 1965), 65.

7. "Pathological": Abigail Ann Hamblen, "Henry James and the Freedom Fighters of the Seventies," *Georgia Review*, Spring 1966, 36; "love for Basil": Mildred E. Hartsock, "Henry James and the Cities of the Plain," *Modern Language Quarterly*, September 1968, 303; Louise Bogan, "*The Bostonians*" (1945), in *Poet's Alphabet* (New York, 1970), 243, 244; Fetterly, *Resisting Reader*, 109.

8. Fetterly, *ibid.*, 131, 134, 137. Verena's oppressor: Robert Emmet Long, *Henry James: The Early Novels* (Boston, 1983), 148, 198f; "dogmatist": Janet A. Gabler, "James's Rhetorical Arena: The Metaphor of Battle in *The Bostonians*," *Texas Studies in Literature and Language*, Fall 1985, 285; "frightening": Merla Wolk, "Family Plot in *The Bostonians*: Silencing the Artist's Voice," *Henry James Review*, Winter 1989, 54.

9. "Phallic" critics, "primitive fear," and "biggest phallic gun": Fetterly, *Resisting Reader*, 101, 108, 111–112.

10. "Perverse forces": *ibid.*, 112; "evidence": *ibid.*, 110.

11. Among critics accepting Fetterly's reading is John Carlos Rowe, *The Theoretical Dimensions of Henry James* (Madison, Wisc., 1984).

12. Fetterly, *Resisting Reader*, 115.

13. On the range of interpretations of Ransom see *ibid.*, 111; Theodore C. Miller, "The Muddled Politics of Henry James's *The Bostonians*," *Georgia Review*, 1972, 343; Joan Maxwell, "Delighting in a Bite: James's Seduction of His Readers in *The Bostonians*," *Journal of Narrative Technique*, Winter 1988, 19.

14. "Selfish": Edward Wagenknecht, *The Novels of Henry James* (New

York, 1983), 140; also Anne T. Margolis, *Henry James and the Problem of Audience: An International Act* (Ann Arbor, 1985), 67; Lillian Faderman, *Surpassing the Love of Men: Romantic Friendship and Love Between Women from the Renaissance to the Present* (New York, 1981), 193; Philip Page, "The Curious Narration of *The Bostonians*," *American Literature*, November 1974, 378. "Pigheaded": Wagenknecht, *Novels*, 140; "crude": Margolis, *Audience*, 67. "Rigid": Ian F. A. Bell, "Language, Setting, and Self in *The Bostonians*," *Modern Language Quarterly*, September 1988, 214; "a liar": Nina Auerbach, *Communities of Women: An Idea in Fiction* (Cambridge, Mass., 1978), 129; a narcissist: Rowe, *Theoretical Dimensions*, 93; "manipulative": Faderman, *Surpassing*, 193; acts in "bad faith": Mary Suzanne Schriber, *Gender and the Writer's Imagination: From Cooper to Wharton* (Lexington, Ky., 1987), 146; "offensive flippancy": Alfred Habegger, *Henry James and the "Woman Business,"* (Cambridge, England, 1989), 202; "infuriating arrogance": Elizabeth McMahan, "Sexual Desire and Illusion in *The Bostonians*," *Modern Fiction Studies*, Summer 1979, 247; a "fool": Schriber, *Gender*, 147. "Male brutality": Judith Wilt, "Desperately Seeking Verena: A Resistant Reading of *The Bostonians*," *Feminist Studies*, Summer 1987, 303; "right-stuff brutality": Habegger, "*Woman Business*," 195; "brutal hunger for success": Wilt, "Verena," 303. "Dogged cruelty": Sara deSaussure Davis, "*The Bostonians* Reconsidered," in Donald Pizer, ed., *Essays in American Literature in Memory of Richard P. Adams* (New Orleans, 1978), 56; "sadism": Auerbach, *Communities*, 207n, and Fetterly, *Resisting Reader*, 145; "hypocrite and tyrant": Davis, "*Bostonians*," 55; "enslaver": Millicent Bell, *Meaning in Henry James* (Cambridge, Mass., 1991), 138.

15. "Satanic effect": Josephine Hendin, "What Verena Knew," *New Republic* (July 16, 23, 1984), 28; "abduction" and "virtual rape": Rowe, *Theoretical Dimensions*, 99; "rape": Habegger, "*Woman Business*," 195; "murder": Alison Lurie, "A Fine Romance," *New York Review of Books*, April 25, 1991, 24; "assassination": Davis, "*Bostonians*," 55, and Faderman, *Surpassing*, 193; "beserker fury": Habegger, "*Woman Business*," 195; "contaminates": Auerbach, *Communities*, 129; "everything...that charmed": Hendin, "What Verena Knew," 29.

16. "Retracted": Maxwell, "Delighting in a Bite," 31n. Attacks on Anderson: Fetterly, *Resisting Reader*, 110, and Davis, "*Bostonians*," 51.

17. Charles R. Anderson, Introduction to *The Bostonians* (London, 1984, 1986), 26.

18. Alfred Habegger, Introduction to *The Bostonians* (Indianapolis, 1976), xix–xx (his italics), xxiv–xxv.

19. Habegger, *"Woman Business,"* 218. "Feminist revisionist": quoted from *"Woman Business"* in book review by Philip Horne, *Essays in Criticism* (July 1991), 269. "Essential anti-feminism": Habegger, "Henry James's *Bostonians* and the Fiction of Democratic Vulgarity," in Ian F. A. Bell and D. K. Adams, eds., *American Literary Landscapes: The Fiction and the Fact* (London, 1988); "authoritarianism" and "sinister design": *ibid.*, 120. For a similar reading, in which James is said to seduce the liberal reader, see Christopher Butler, Introduction to *The Bostonians* (New York, 1992), ix.

20. "Resist," "sneering," etc.: Habegger, *"Woman Business,"* 221, 219, 185, 189. "Historicizing": Habegger, "Democratic Vulgarity," 120. For other feminists' usage see Davis, *"Bostonians,"* 40; Wilt, "Verena," 294; and compare Bell, *Meaning in Henry James*, 147. "Life of its own": Habegger, *"Woman Business,"* 209.

21. "Conservatism": Habegger, "Democratic Vulgarity," 113; "masculinist instinct": Wilt, "Verena," 314.

22. "Hysterical attack": Margolis, *Problem of Audience*, 68. "Prolixity": Davis, *"Bostonians,"* 39; "undisciplined expression": Michael Anesko, *"Friction with the Market": Henry James and the Profession of Authorship* (New York, 1986), 100. For summaries of other attacks on James's artistry see Maxwell, "Delighting in a Bite," 31n, and Daniel Heaton, "The Altered Characterization of Miss Birdseye in Henry James's *The Bostonians,"* *American Literature*, January 1979, 588n. Also compare Susan Mizruchi, "The Politics of Temporality in Henry James's *The Bostonians," Nineteenth-Century Fiction*, September 1985, 213, and Page, "Curious Narration," 378. Earlier dissatisfactions with *The Bostonians* are noted by Long, *The Early Novels*, 131.

23. "Worries": Page, "Curious Narration," 378; "timidly equivocates": Mizruchi, "Politics of Temporality," 213; "draws back" and "refusing... epiphany," Bell, *Meaning in Henry James*, 141. James as uneasy: Butler, Introduction, xii; "impotent": Mizruchi, "Politics of Temporality," 214; "becomes oppressed": Stuart Hutchinson, *Henry James: An American as Modernist* (New York, 1982), 54.

24. "Decline": Hendin, "What Verena Knew," 28; "defeated": David Howard, *"The Bostonians,"* in *The Air of Reality: New Essays on Henry James* (London, 1972), 76; "terrible fate": Faderman, *Surpassing*, 192; "nature's ploy": McMahan, "Sexual Desire," 249.

25. "Can only explain": Page, "Curious Narration," 377; "wrenches her": Margolis, *Audience*, 67; "more vicious" vs. "healthy": Rowe, *Theoretical Dimensions*, 91.

26. "Person he 'loves'": Davis, *"Bostonians,"* 46; "Olive's tutelage": Faderman, *Surpassing*, 194; "advantages with Olive": Wagenknecht, *Novels of Henry James*, 105.

27. "Oppressor": Long, *Early Novels*, 149; "captivity": Wagenknecht, *Novels of Henry James*, 105. "More vicious": Rowe, *Theoretical Dimensions*, 91. Critics who equate Olive and Ransom include Fetterly, *Resisting Reader*, 146; Page, "Curious Narration," 377–378; Catherine Stimpson, "The Case of Miss Joan Didion," *Ms.* magazine, January 1973, 41; Hendin, "What Verena Knew," 29. "Normal" is put in quotation marks by Auerbach, *Communities*, 120.

28. "Sad fact," "doomed," and threat to "human potential": Millicent Bell, "The Bostonian Story," *Partisan Review* (2/1985), 119, 113, 114; "ill suited": McMahan, "Sexual Desire," 250; "perversity" (italicized in original): Rowe, *Theoretical Dimensions*, 89; "power relationships," and "predictable fall": Maxwell, "Delighting in a Bite," 21, 28.

29. *Ibid.*, 19.

30. Bogan, *"The Bostonians,"* 246.

31. Wilt, "Verena," 304.

32. "Romantic conventions": R. D. Gooder, Introduction to *The Bostonians* (New York, 1984), xxx. On romance conventions in *The Bostonians* see especially Long, *Early Novels*, 146. Fetterly, *Resisting Reader*, 128.

33. Weak of character: Wolk, "Family Plot," 56; "of little value," and "vacuous" speeches: Schriber, *Gender*, 147; "fool": Sallie J. Hall, "Henry James and the Bluestockings: Satire and Morality in *The Bostonians*," in Donna G. Fricke and Douglas C. Fricke, eds., *Aeolian Harps: Essays in Literature in Honor of Maurice Browning Cramer* (Bowling Green, Ohio, 1976), 214.

34. "Resistant" rewriting and "integrity as a feminist": Wilt, "Verena," 294, 312, quoting Davis, *"Bostonians."* "Repressions of the past": Mizruchi; "Politics of Temporality," 211. For a related feminist critical method see Butler, Introduction, xiii.

35. This line is emphasized in the analysis by Lyall H. Powers, *Henry James: An Introduction and Interpretation* (New York, 1970), 80. "Absently utters": Anesko, "Friction with the Market," 98.

36. Howe, Introduction, vi–vii, xiii, vi, vii.

37. Anderson, Introduction, 29; Howe, Introduction, vi; "awful earnestness": Peter Buitenhuis, *The Grasping Imagination: The American Writings of Henry James* (Toronto, 1970), 159.

38. Fetterly, *Resisting Reader*, 131.

39. See Trilling, *"The Bostonians,"* 102.

Appendix: *Typee*

1. David Williams, "Peeping Tommo: *Typee* as Satire," *Canadian Review of American Studies* 6 (Spring 1975), 46.

2. Edgar A. Dryden, *Melville's Thematics of Form: The Great Art of Telling the Truth* (Baltimore, 1968). The chapter on *Typee* is printed—along with early reviews, other essays, a bibliography of writings on *Typee*, and an introductory survey of *Typee* criticism by the editor—in Milton R. Stern, ed., *Critical Essays on Herman Melville's "Typee"* (Boston, 1982). The quotations are from Stern, 181.

3. "Historical Note" by Leon Howard and "Note on the Text" by the editors, in *Typee*, vol. 1 of *The Writings of Herman Melville*, ed. by Harrison Hayford, Herschel Parker, and G. Thomas Tanselle (Evanston, Ill., 1968), 288, 315.

4. See Herman Melville to John Murray, July 30, 1846, in Merrell R. Davis and William H. Gilman, eds., *The Letters of Herman Melville* (New Haven, 1960), 43–44. Melville's letters cited below are from the same source.

5. Chase's discussion from *Herman Melville: A Critical Study* (New York, 1949) is reprinted in Stern, *Critical Essays*; Stern's discussion, also reprinted in his anthology, is from *The Fine Hammered Steel of Herman Melville* (Urbana, Ill., 1957).

6. Williams, "Peeping Tommo," 47. Mitchell Breitweiser, "False Sympathy in Melville's *Typee*," *American Quarterly* 34 (Fall 1982), 416–417. Thomas J. Scorza, "Tragedy in the State of Nature: Melville's *Typee*," *Interpretation* 8 (January 1979), reprinted in Stern, *Critical Essays*, 239–240.

7. Williams, "Peeping Tommo," 43, 42. Rogin, *Subversive Genealogy*, 48.

8. Ziff, *Literary Democracy*, 5. Louise K. Barnett, *The Ignoble Savage: American Literary Racism, 1790–1890* (Westport, Conn., 1975), 173.

9. Joyce Sparer Adler, *"Typee* and *Omoo*: Of 'Civilized' War or 'Savage' Peace," in her *War in Melville's Imagination*, reprinted in Stern, *Critical Essays*, 245.

10. Barnett, *Literary Racism*, 173–174. John Wenke, "Melville's *Typee*: A Tale of Two Worlds," in Stern, *Critical Essays*, 254. Ziff, *Literary Democracy*, 3.

11. Rogin, *Subversive Genealogy*, 47; Ziff, *Literary Democracy*, 3.

12. The five critics are: T. Walter Herbert, Jr., *Marquesan Encounters: Melville and the Meaning of Civilization* (Cambridge, Mass., 1980), 165; Williams, "Peeping Tommo," 37; Ziff, *Literary Democracy*, 10; Rogin, *Subversive Genealogy*, 48; and Karcher, *Shadow over the Promised Land*, 4.

13. William Torrey, *Torrey's Narrative* (Boston, 1848).

14. Breitweiser, "False Sympathy," 405, 411.

15. Ralph Linton, "Marquesan Culture," in Abram Kardiner, ed., *The Individual and His Society: The Psychodynamics of Primitive Social Organizations* (New York, 1939, 1955), 181. Additional details of Typee life not directly footnoted come from the following books: Robert C. Suggs, *The Hidden Worlds of Polynesia: The Chronicle of an Archaeological Expedition to Nuku Hiva in the Marquesas Islands* (New York, 1962), and *Marquesan Sexual Behavior* (New York, 1966); Herbert, *Marquesan Encounters*; and Greg Dening, ed., *The Marquesan Journal of Edward Roberts, 1797–1824* (Honolulu, 1974). For Melville's anthropological knowledge see Charles R. Anderson, *Melville in the South Seas* (New York, 1939).

16. Suggs, *Hidden Worlds*, 44.

17. Adler, "*Typee* and *Omoo*," 247.

18. Breitweiser, "False Sympathy," 407, 396.

INDEX

Abel, Darrel, 31–32, 34

Adventures of Huckleberry Finn,
16, 100–126; and American
Indians, 118; antislavery
interpretation, 102–105,
108, 117, 123; black critics
vs. white, 113–114,
121–122; and capitalism,
118; censorship of,
100–101; critics of 1950s,
101–102; critics of 1960s,
107–108; critics of 1980s,
108–126; and the family,
118–119; final chapters of,
103–105, 124–125; and
genteelism, 101–102, 110,
123; instrumental
interpretation, 117–118,
123; as literary realism, 101;
myth vs. social consciousness
interpretations, 104, 105;
plot of, 102–103;
Reconstruction reading of,
114–116, 123; as

repudiation of Civil War,
22, 120

Ahab (character): as
authoritarian, 50; and
railroads, 67–68; as robber
baron, 51; totalitarian
tendencies, 56–57

Allegory: *Billy Budd* as, 77–78;
Moby Dick as, 48–49

American ideology: in service
of evil, 14

American Literary Scholarship,
61

*American Novel and Its
Tradition* (Chase), 158

American Renaissance
(Matthiessen), 50

Anderson, Charles R.,
134–135, 146

Anthropology: and double
standards, 171; and Typeean
culture, 165–171

Arac, Jonathan, 14–15

"Art of Fiction" (James), 148

Index

Index